Cloud
Walkers

Cloud Walkers

Six Climbs on Major Canadian Peaks

PADDY SHERMAN

Maps by John A. Hall

1965 ST. MARTIN'S PRESS NEW YORK

The poem 'Breathless', from *Poems* by Wilfrid Noyce,
is reprinted by permission of William Heinemann Ltd.

Library of Congress Catalogue Card No. 65-25069

Printed in Canada

Contents

Preface / vii

Mount Logan: Mightiest Hump of Nature / 1
    Map on pages 6-7

Mount Waddington: Nightmare Moulded in Rock / 39
    Map on page vi

Mount Slesse: an Air Liner Vanishes / 60

Mount Robson: the Dangerous Mountain / 92

A Great Climber Dies: a Hiker Lives / 112

Mount Fairweather: Ice-Cliff and Earthquake / 132
    Map on page x

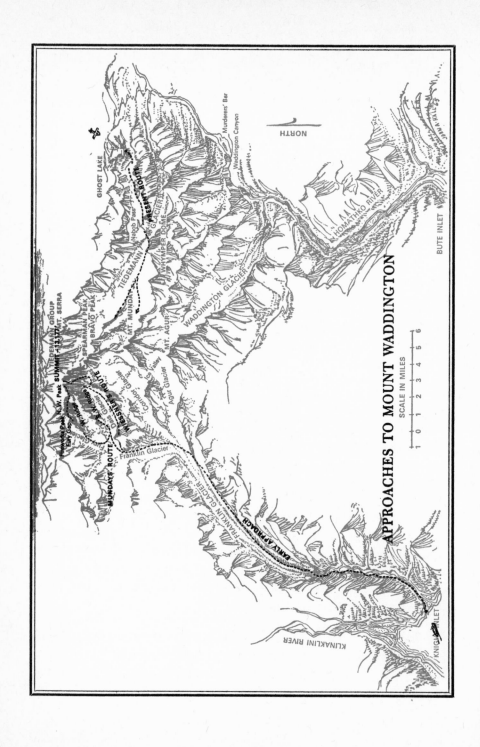

APPROACHES TO MOUNT WADDINGTON

Preface

The western limits of Canada are buttressed by some of the mightiest mountain ranges on earth. Running north-west from the United States border, a thousand miles of mountains serrate the Pacific rim to the boundary of the Yukon. These are wild and lonely mountains, little known, less travelled. They soar from the sea to 15,300 feet.

At the Yukon border they merge with the giants of Alaska and become almost Himalayan in scale, Arctic in character. In this section, Canada's mountains culminate in Mount Logan, 19,850 feet high and one of the world's great summits. Its massif is so big that it is a range in itself.

There is more, much more. The mountain wall along the Pacific Ocean bounds British Columbia. That province covers 366,255 square miles; more than 75 per cent of it is at an elevation of 3,000 feet or higher. As you travel from west to east you encounter one great range after another, ending in the Rocky Mountains which sprawl over an area 850 miles long running north-west from the U.S. border.

Such mountains have produced great feats from many men, tales of triumph and lonely terror, of delight and swift disaster. Few of these stories have been adequately told, although some are epic in the old and undiluted meaning of the word.

Since 1906 members of the Alpine Club of Canada have explored and climbed among these mountains. Each year the club has published its journal, recording – mainly between the lines – feats that easily match those in the other and better-known great ranges of the world.

I have drawn on those journals for details of some of the earlier great climbs, and wish to thank the club. Particularly, I thank the editor of the *Canadian Alpine Journal*, Mrs. W. A. D. Munday, herself one of the great figures in Canadian mountaineering history, for her encouragement.

She knows as well as I that these earlier feats are too fine to be kept for the esoteric pleasure of the addict. There is much in them to make a larger audience proud.

P.S.

Photographs

Starting opposite page 84

MOUNT LOGAN – *fluted south-east ridge (1); Logan Glacier (2).*

MOUNT WADDINGTON – *Tiedemann Glacier (3); summit spire (4); Bravo Col (5).*

MOUNT SLESSE – *wreckage on face of precipice (6); wreckage dangling from control cable (7).*

MOUNT ROBSON – *viewed from the east (8); near summit (9); South-east Shoulder (10).*

MOUNT SEYMOUR – *the rescue (11); viewed from Vancouver (12).*

MOUNT FAIRWEATHER – *High Camp (13); ice towers (14); Lituya Bay (15); crevassed glaciers (16); dangerous crevasses (17).*

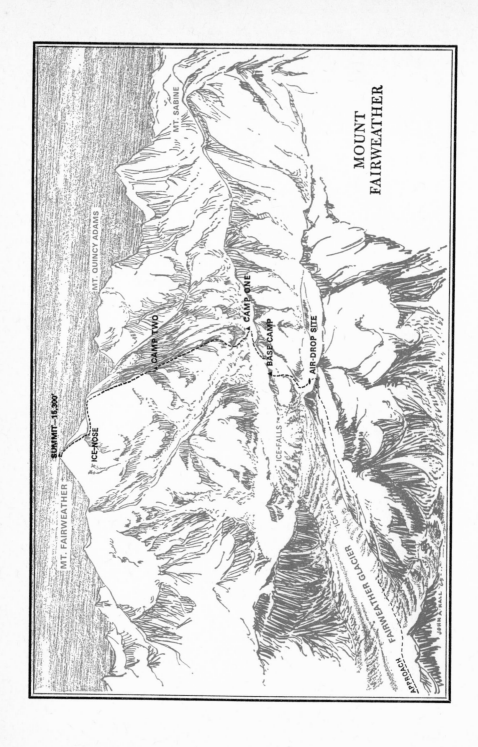

MOUNT
FAIRWEATHER

MT. FAIRWEATHER
SUMMIT—15,300'
ICE-NOSE
MT. QUINCY ADAMS
MT. SABINE
CAMP TWO
CAMP ONE
BASE CAMP
ICE-FALLS
AIR-DROP SITE
ICE-FALLS
ICE-FALLS
FAIRWEATHER GLACIER
APPROACH

JOHN A. HALL. '65

Cloud
Walkers

Mightiest Hump
of Nature

MOUNT LOGAN

Map on pages 6-7

Mount Logan, some two hundred miles west of Whitehorse in the Yukon Territory, is Canada's highest peak; it soars to 19,850 feet, a scant 450 feet lower than Alaska's Mount McKinley, the apex of North America. Twelve years after the first ascent of McKinley, in 1913, Logan was the highest unclimbed peak on the North American continent: the highest, and perhaps the toughest, for in its eternal armour of snow and ice, and in the grim ferocity of its defences, it is no mean match for Everest itself.

Many of the world's great peaks are taller than Logan. But it is a coastal mountain, rising almost from the sea, not from a Tibetan plateau 15,000 feet above sea-level. Glaciers from its base flow right to the Pacific Ocean. If Logan's uplift above its base were to be super-imposed on a Tibetan interior plateau, it would rank with Everest. And seldom is there found a single mountain massif with Logan's monumental bulk. It measures 100 miles around at the base, a snow-white fang protruding from 25,000 square miles of ice that constitute the biggest glacial area in the world apart from the Antarctic and Greenland.

I

If the mountain could be sliced off at the 16,000-foot level, which is higher than Europe's loftiest peak, the resulting plateau would cover thirty square miles. Its many-toothed summit ridges, twenty miles long and 3,000 miles farther north than Everest, are a cosmic comb, raking the moisture from countless year-round storms spawned in the far Pacific. The result is astonishing.

On the cold north side of Everest, eternal snow and ice stretch down to the 16,500-foot level, giving a vertical snow-and-ice region of 12,500 feet. The comparable zone on Logan covers 16,000 feet, and the summit broods, remote and frightening, a clear 14,000 feet above the general level of the surrounding glaciers. At the time of the first attempt on Logan, the nearest habitation was 150 miles away, and the approach included almost eighty miles of glaciers on which no man had ever set foot.

The first recorded sighting of the giant mountain was by Israel C. Russell of the United States Geological Survey. In 1890, he was trying to make the first ascent of Mount St. Elias (18,008 feet), then believed to be the highest peak in Alaska. He didn't reach the peak but he did spot Mount Logan, twenty-six miles away. He reported his find this way: "The clouds parted towards the northeast, revealing several giant peaks not before seen, some of which seem to rival St. Elias itself. One stranger rising in three white domes far above the clouds was especially magnificent. As this was probably the first time its summit was ever seen, we took the liberty of giving it a name. It will appear on our maps as Mt. Logan, in honour of Sir William E. Logan, founder and for long director of the Geological Survey of Canada."

The fame of Mount St. Elias had spread throughout the world, and in 1897 the Duke of the Abruzzi, one of the most colourful figures in mountaineering history, travelled there from Italy. With his vast retinue of Italian guides and porters, he climbed the peak.

His famous personal photographer, Quintino Sella, took from the summit the first photographs of Logan. They showed mile after mile of seemingly impossible precipices and ice-falls. In 1913, H. F. Lambart of the Canadian Geological Survey decided from his triangulations that Logan, almost astride the Yukon-Alaska border, was in fact not an Alaskan giant but Canada's highest mountain.

In 1913, Albert H. MacCarthy and William Wasbrough Foster were also making a big contribution to Canadian mountaineering history: they made the first ascent of Mount Robson (12,972 feet), then believed to be the highest peak in Canada outside the Yukon. As they celebrated the event around an Alpine Club of Canada camp-fire, the club's director, A. O. Wheeler (whose son, later Sir Oliver Wheeler, was to be surveyor on the first Mount Everest expedition in 1921), proposed that Mount Logan should be climbed. Plans were started at once, but had to be abandoned when the war came.

In 1923, Albert MacCarthy, now a captain in the United States Navy, was appointed leader of the expedition, and he soon realized just what he was in for. The mountain's "stupendous bulk", he said, after a lot of research, made it "the mightiest hump of nature in the western hemisphere if not the largest in the world".

There were three possible approaches: from Yakutat Bay on the coast; from Kluane Lake on the north-east; or from McCarthy, Alaska, which was to the north-west. Yakutat Bay was ruled out almost at once. Although the Duke of the Abruzzi had used it for St. Elias, the area was notoriously stormy and dangerous. There was no satisfactory base there then, and the approach wound up the wrong side of the mountain. The Kluane Lake route, which is today crossed by the Alaska Highway, then involved a stretch of sixty miles that was completely unexplored. It was obvious to MacCarthy that whichever way he tried to reach the mountain he was in for many problems. So, instead of attempting to climb it in 1924, he decided to spend a season on reconnaissance, concentrating on the route from the village of McCarthy.

This meant an eighty-six-mile trek alongside the Chitina River, an unpredictable glacier-fed stream – one moment peacefully murmuring among the rocks, the next hurling giant boulders about like peas, and fighting to burst from its low, confining banks. Apart from winter, the only time a climbing party could use it safely would be in the slack spell between the early run-off from melting snow and the main run-off caused by melting on the billions of tons of glacier ice.

With Andrew M. Taylor and Miles (Scotty) Atkinson, two McCarthy guides, Captain MacCarthy made a thirty-seven-day trip up the Chitina and over the fifty-two miles of ice beyond it to Cascade, the logical site for base camp. Despite a tremendous amount of work, they

3

were frustrated by bad weather, and the farthest point they reached was eighteen miles from the peak and only 10,200 feet in altitude. But he made the decision: tough as it was, this was at least a possible way to get onto the mountain. From there, the mountaineers would have to make their own way.

It was obvious to him that if they were to have a chance of reaching the summit the climbers must arrive on the mountain in good condition, not exhausted by carrying in tons of supplies. So it was proposed, almost casually, in the way of men of forceful action, that the supplies should be taken in and cached during the coming winter.

This feat in itself was worthy of comparison with Antarctic sledging epics, and it is still considered one of the greatest winter freighting jobs ever tackled in that wild and inhospitable border country.

It began in February 1925, at the height of an exceptionally cold winter in the valley, with everything buried deep under an unusually heavy snowfall. Almost three and a half tons of supplies had to be taken in for the climbers to allow them to make an extended siege of Logan. A ton of hay and oats had to be transported for the climbing party's pack-horses, as no grass would be growing when the assault got under way in May. On top of all this, the freighting party itself needed more than five tons of supplies for its three-month task. To move this total of ten tons a distance of some 150 miles over frozen river-beds and tumbling glaciers, a party of six men was chosen, with six horses and three teams of seven sled dogs.

From February 4 to February 13, Andy Taylor and Austin Trim, with six horses, broke trail up the first forty-five miles of the Chitina Valley. Often the temperature went down to −45°F.; once it dropped to a paralysing −52°. Despite this, the two big bobsleds pulled by six horses left McCarthy at 9 a.m. on February 17. Two hours later, the wildly excited dogs hauled their sledges along McCarthy's main street and down to the frozen river at a run. The fight was formally on.

The route along the river-beds was longer than the land trail, but had the great benefit for the heavily loaded horses that it was generally at an easy gradient. Much of Alaska's heavy freighting is done in winter, when turbulent rivers turn, by the physics of frost, into wide, strong highways. This has its problems, of course. When the equivalent of a highway pot-hole appears, the results are likely to be calamitous, with a team plunging through a hole into the still-flowing water beneath.

MacCarthy's party had no serious trouble on the first day's march of sixteen miles, which took them to the junction of the Chitina and Nizina rivers. But they did have to flounder through patches where the water had overflowed and was covered by only an inch or two of ice. Often the party sank down into water ten inches deep. Combined with stretches of seemingly bottomless, fluffy snow, this did not help the unconditioned muscles of men and beasts. That night, rather than jam with the others into a two-man cabin, MacCarthy put up his tent in a snow-bank and slept snugly.

The snow-storm that began next morning was just the start of weather problems that plagued them from there on. Nature seemed to have got everything backwards, MacCarthy complained. Because of the bitterly cold winter, the river level was low and the sleds often had to be hauled over boulder-strewn gravel bars. Despite the cold, stretches of open water often appeared, forcing them to make difficult detours. And, when they reached stretches that they knew should be good, insurmountable ice jams, piled high by the tremendous pressure of the river, confronted them.

The dogs somehow seemed to thrive on the difficult conditions. They always had enough energy to start a furious fight at the least little chance. On the second day of the trip, Driver, leading one team, set too fast a pace for a team-mate known as Scotty Dog. Scotty attacked Driver from behind and with a sudden slash bit out his left eye. There was nothing the men could do for the poor dog, but as it seemed reluctant to lie down and die they left it in the harness. Time and again Driver licked his paw and then rubbed the wound. Within a week, it had healed completely. MacCarthy marvelled: "What would have happened to one of us had we sustained such an injury and received such scant treatment? Dumb animals are possessed of much that men must envy."

But there was not much to envy about the horses. For thirteen days it was impossible to take off their harness. It was frozen solid. And in the mornings, it was not hard to be sorry for both horses and dogs. To make the most of the daylight, early starts were important. Yet day after day they had to wait until 10 a.m. because the early air was so cold that the deep breathing needed for the hard work of hauling would have frozen the lungs of all the animals. The carefully planned schedule fell apart. But by February 27 they reached Hubrick's Camp, the ramshackle home of a former prospector at the head of Chitina

5

SUMMIT—19,850′ BIVOUAC FIRST PEAK PLATEAU CAMP CAMP 18-5

Yakutat Bay

MOUNT LOGAN WINDY CAMP ICE-CLIFF CAMP

KING COLING CAMP

KING COLING PEAK MT. ST. ELIA

KING King Trench OBSERVATION CAMP

GLACIER Quartz Ridge CASCADE

YUKON TERRITORY

ADVANCE BASE CACHE

NORTH

OGILVIE GLACIER

TURN CAMP

ICE-CAMP NO. 3

LOGAN GLACIER Climbers' Route ICE-CAMP NO

BOUNDARY CAMP

WALSH GLACIER

MOUNT LOGAN

SCALE IN MILES

4   0   4   8   12

PACIFIC OCEAN

ALASKA

INTERNATIONAL BOUNDARY

BALDWIN GLACIER

BALDWIN JUNCTION CAMP

ICE CAMP NO. 1

FRASER BALDWIN CACHE

CAMP

Winter Route

Moraine Mounds

GORGE CAMP

DEVIL'S DOOR

CAMP

Gorge of Fate

CACHE

Climbers' Route

PORTAL CAMP

GLACIER

CHITINA

Winter Route

CHITINA RIVER

TRAIL'S END

HUBRICK'S

JOHN A. HALL

Valley. Barely two miles away was the bush-covered snout of the Chitina Glacier. This growth of bush right out of the ice is one of the most striking oddities of Alaska's giant glaciers. Many of the rivers of ice come right down to sea-level, in a mild and humid climate. Vegetable growth is prolific in the short, warm summer with its almost continuous daylight. Under the circumstances, the coating of rubble old glaciers have gouged from the mountains' flanks is rich enough to produce dense stands of slide alder.

Reaching this point through the deep, soft snow and Arctic cold had brought problems enough, but these were to serve as a mere apprenticeship for the work ahead. This was the end of the "easy" valley stretch; ahead were the perilous gorges and glaciers of the mountain section.

Right in front of them was a major worry. They had to get to the west side of Baldwin Glacier to know they were sure of reaching base camp on Ogilvie Glacier. There were two conceivable ways to get there – along the south side of Chitina and Logan glaciers, or along the north side of Chitina and across it and another glacier to the Logan. The second was obviously impossible for heavy loads, and the first had been abandoned as impossible by Lambart's party when it was surveying the border in 1913.

MacCarthy decided to try the route that the earlier party had abandoned. On February 28, he and Atkinson set out on snow-shoes for the south side of Chitina Glacier, and headed with considerable trepidation up the canyon formed by the steep edge of the ice and the mountain side. MacCarthy went as far as a narrow, impressive cleft between vertical granite cliffs 150 feet high. He called it "The Portal". The summer river boils through here in an angry spate.

Atkinson pushed on and late that night reported that the route was feasible right onto Baldwin Glacier. He cautiously refused to guess at how long it would stay feasible. But before he knew this MacCarthy was working back from The Portal, marking an ice route into the valley. He was not a demonstrative man by nature, but even as he worked he found himself calling the route, in his own mind, "The Gorge of Fate". Some subconscious instinct, with its roots in frequent association with danger, must have been warning him of trouble to come. But even this did not tell him how near the whole party would come to catastrophe.

There were more stretches of open water, and the very next day the

8

ice-bridge spanning the first of these collapsed. Logs were hauled in to make a new bridge. By March 5, the entire load of supplies was cached four miles beyond The Portal. This was the limit at which the heavy horses could work. Already there had been problems with their weight on the sometimes flimsy ice-bridges. Next day the horses went back to McCarthy, and the rest of the party headed another two and a half miles up-stream to find a final, safe camp where everything could be stored.

The final part of the gorge was by far the most dangerous. Here the tumbling cataract raced along, and many patches of open water leered up at them, inviting the misstep that would promptly bury them under the solid ice a few yards down-stream. Often the only way to go was on a fringe of ice still sticking to the steep rock-wall. A few feet to the side, the torrent gradually undermined their road. One piece especially bothered them — the last apparent danger on the route. This was a ten-foot slit in granite cliffs "which because of its narrowness, its latent dangers and the satanic appearance of an ice pinnacle that seemed to stand guard over it, we called the Devil's Door".

On March 6, they set up Gorge Camp beyond these dangers. Next day, while MacCarthy stayed to wash the dishes, the others left with the dogs to start the dangerous business of hauling heavy sledges of supplies through on the inadequate bridges.

The temperature was still around 25° below zero, and Gorge Camp was a frigid, cheerless place under its shroud of snow. Yet they dreaded the thought that the warmth and new hope of spring were on the way. With warmth would come weakness. Already the ice was showing signs of deterioration. Would it last long enough for them to finish the job? If they could not get the supplies through here now, the expedition would not be able to start for at least another year. It would be impossible to follow this route with loads in summer.

It was this urgent undercurrent of haste that sent MacCarthy quickly through the camp chores that morning. Then he hurried on down to help at the bottle-neck wooden bridge. Here, each sledge-load had to be unpacked, carried across item by item, and then loaded again on the other side. Within a few minutes, the worries he wouldn't admit fully even to himself came true.

The dog-teams were coming back — the sledges empty and defeat scrawled dully in the haggard, bearded faces of the men.

9

Andy Taylor told him, "The Devil's Door is shut. The ice we crossed on yesterday is ten feet under water. The trail for 200 yards up-stream is now twenty feet down at the bottom of a lake."

Almost everything they had was stored in the cache below the blockage. There was no food in camp for the dogs, and practically none for the men.

The dogs were immediately taken back to camp and tied up, and by 10.30 a.m. MacCarthy, Taylor, and Atkinson set off on snow-shoes to try to find a way down to the supplies. They crossed the river up-stream, struggled onto the glacier, and then, in five hours of desperately hard work, outflanked the door. They felt it would have been impossible to get the loaded dogs through by this route. Inching slowly back into the gorge below the Devil's Door, they soon found the cause of the trouble.

It was simple but spectacular: thousands of tons of ice had broken from the towering glacier-wall and filled the bottom of the gorge. The speeding river was stopped, and it rapidly backed up into a lake. But the current was fortunately still at work. Already the surging water had cut a small channel through the ice-jam. By the time the tired men were ready to pack their loads of food back, the gorge was passable again.

The warning was obvious, and they took note of it. Next morning they were out at dawn. Taylor and MacCarthy hacked at the ice-jam with axes and shovels, clearing a narrow, reasonably smooth route for the dogs. Atkinson and Henry Olsen started rushing supplies up to the wooden bridge, using twenty-one dogs on the two sledges. As they made repeated trips to the bridge, there was ever-increasing need for haste: the slabs of ice on which the logs were resting were being noticeably eaten away by the rushing water.

They worked until dark. As Taylor brought the loads from the bridge, he found things rapidly nearing the impossible stage at the door. Their original trail had followed a fringe of ice along the southern wall. But this had now broken off, and its northern side was under water. It was still possible to cross it, though it lay on its side, but the angle was steepening as the water worried away at the edges.

Even the dogs were frightened by its obvious threat. They cringed, tails down, as they approached, and slid along it on their bellies. Some of the dogs refused to cross it at all, and had to be dragged by their drivers. With every trip, the tension increased; there was much to be done yet, but if the bridge went out, so would their plans.

It went at 6.30 that night. A quiet crack as if it was weary of holding out so long, and the slab sank slowly into the hurrying waters. But the last load was through – less than five minutes before. The tension cracked too, and the men found themselves laughing, almost involuntarily – cheering and pounding each other on the back.

This was no time for rest and relaxation, however. They were far behind schedule and still had several glaciers to negotiate. Day after day they toiled. First move a load; then dump it and go back for more. Dump this just past the first, and go back for more – and more and more and more. Soon every tiny detail of their snow-white world became monotonously familiar. But it was never so familiar that they could quite forget the danger they were in. The route was often covered with the debris of huge ice-blocks hurled down by the glacier in seeming defiance.

MacCarthy wrote: "No matter how long and how hard we worked, the task seemed to be unending. But we had had the temerity to undertake the job and there was no help for us. We must carry on and see it through to some sort of finish."

On March 12, he almost came to a premature sort of finish. As he prospected alone for a sledge route on the glacier, he became hopelessly lost in a blizzard. At one stage he found he had walked in a complete circle, despite his long experience. He tried to retrace his tracks, but the wind had wiped them out. It was getting dark, and he was preparing to spend the night out when he recognized the ice-pinnacle standing guard at the Devil's Door. The ogre of foreboding that had frightened him when first he saw it was his salvation now. He knew where he was: on top of towering, dangerous ice-cliffs only a mile below the camp. It was dark as he climbed slowly down the cliffs and back to camp.

The temperature was almost 30° below zero that night and the storm raged unabated. But, since most things in life are relative, Albert MacCarthy curled up in his sleeping-bag on his bed of boulders, shuddered at the thought of being lost, and spent the most comfortable night he could ever remember.

From here the going became progressively rougher. On some steep stretches the dogs could barely pull even a light load. Slowly, exhausted by hard work and monotony, they crossed the Baldwin Glacier and started towards the open, easy-looking flat stretches of Logan Glacier.

Before they could reach it, though, they had to cross three miles of moraine — a jumbled, senseless tangle of boulders gouged from the cliffs by the irresistible ice and piled in millions of tons across their path. It was March 31 before they finally set up camp in the middle of the smooth white face of Logan Glacier, pitching the tents three feet deep in a bank of snow. The slow-motion rush went on, step by step, up the Logan Glacier and onto the Ogilvie. On April 13, two and a half tons of equipment, comprising the whole advance base camp the climbers would use, was stored nine miles up the Ogilvie. All the meat and other uncanned foods likely to attract bears, wolves, or wolverines were carefully stowed in the centre of a huge mound. The whole thing was covered with heavy tarpaulins, and weighted down with rocks and cases of gasoline for their stoves.

They took photographs of the cache in relation to prominent landmarks so that the climbers would be able to find it, and on April 14 the party ran for home. They reached McCarthy on April 26, having been forced to take a different route to get around the Devil's Door. Even travelling light, they took five days to negotiate twenty miles there, proving to their satisfaction that the job would have been impossible with heavy loads.

Under Arctic conditions and in dangerous country, the winter party had travelled over 950 miles in ten weeks, and cached in various key places the four and a half tons of food and equipment without which the ambitious assault on Mount Logan could not even begin.

Should the summit expedition fail, it would be no fault of theirs. Their exploit is still without equal as a mountaineering preliminary, despite the great exploration that has been done in some of the world's highest and most remote ranges. It fittingly prepared the way for one of the world's great feats of mountaineering, which today is almost unknown though it qualifies as perhaps the most outstanding epic of endurance in Canada's rich and vibrant frontier history.

It was the springboard that launched six mountaineers on the way to one of the loneliest places on earth — to the brink of life, that little-known limit where the body abandons the fight and only the prodding of the brain keeps death away.

MacCarthy was waiting on the dock at Cordova when the steamer arrived on May 7, 1925, bringing the climbing party from a trip along a thousand miles of some of the world's most spectacular coast. The official party consisted of MacCarthy himself as leader, Foster, Fred Lambart (deputy leader), and Allen Carpé, who represented the American Alpine Club. It was an unusual group. Lambart was the man who first measured the mountain. MacCarthy, of Annapolis, Maryland, and Wilmer, British Columbia, was forty-nine. So was Lieutenant-Colonel Foster, a former deputy-minister of public works for British Columbia, holder of the Distinguished Service Order and two bars. Allen Carpé, thirty-one, was a research scientist in radio and telegraph, and one of America's best exploratory mountaineers.

At this time, mountaineering was going through one of its most popular phases in Europe and North America. The series of British assaults on Everest, culminating in the tragic death of Mallory and Irvine in 1924, had focused public attention on great feats of exploratory mountaineering. After 1924, the Dalai Lama of Tibet closed his country to climbers. As a result, the climbers of the world turned their eyes to the Alaska region and Logan, in its way as remote and challenging as Everest itself. The American Alpine Club eagerly helped the Alpine Club of Canada organize the assault. It formed its own fund-raising committee, which raised much of the $11,500 that the expedition cost.

It provided something else, equally important: strong recruits for the climbing party. Many United States mountaineers had volunteered to pay their own expenses and help in any way requested if only they could be taken on the trip. On this basis, three outstanding United States climbers now arrived on the steamer. They were Henry S. Hall, Jr., of Boston, R. M. Morgan of Dartmouth College in New Hampshire, and Norman H. Read of Manchester, Massachussetts. Hall, later president of the American Alpine Club, became one of the best and most experienced climbers in the United States and made many difficult expeditions in British Columbia's wild and difficult Coast Range. These men brought the climbing party to seven. To them were added Andy Taylor as transport officer, and H. M. Laing, a naturalist who stayed at Hubrick's throughout the expedition and surveyed the wildlife and plants of the Chitina Valley.

They left McCarthy on May 12 and in six days had reached the end of the trail eighty-eight miles away. Even the eighty-pound packs they put on for the first part of the glacier journey did not slow them much — but they were all relieved when they reached Logan Glacier and used sleds instead. On May 26, they reached the final, main cache at 6,050 feet on the Ogilvie. Cascade, the site of their advanced base camp, was clearly visible eight miles away over the ice, and they immediately started to relay the stores there from the tarpaulin-covered mound.

Now at last they were in a truly alpine area, and their very first relay journey to Cascade impressed this on them. A giant avalanche peeled off the walls of ice overlooking Ogilvie and foamed for thousands of feet through the air in a billowing fountain of white. It was lovely, but lethal for anybody near where it fell. For at least ten minutes after it crashed to the glacier with a battle-front roar, clouds of ice-dust from the pulverized blocks went blowing up the glacier.

It was alpine, too, in the fact that early starts were essential. The nights were no longer really dark, and the miles of white snow in every direction magnified even the faint light of midnight. So they were away by 1 a.m. each day, making sure that they could finish at least one trip in comparative ease over the night-frozen surface. Coming back through the soggy snow was unpleasant, but it was not difficult, as the sleds were empty.

Moving the supplies took five days, and by May 31 they were established in their advanced base camp. It was 7,800 feet above sea-level and took the name of Cascade Camp from the cataract of a splendid ice-fall that tumbled a branch of King Glacier to the Ogilvie.

If a glacier is likened to a river, then the ice-fall is the counterpart of the rapids. A sudden drop in elevation speeds and disrupts the smooth flow, and the tortured ice fractures and splinters in all directions. Blocks as big as skyscrapers fall often, dwarfed in the giant perspective of the peaks. Each looses a roar to match its majesty, and rarely is there peace in the ever-moving ice-fall. Even then it is at best a patchwork truce, shattered by the sporadic crack and rattle of dissension as more blocks settle, preparing to leap to their own spectacular ends.

It was an incomparable spot, epic in its scale and beauty, and a perfect psychological stimulant for the mighty task that had now fairly begun.

The stimulant did its job well. During the next two days the eight men carried three-quarters of a ton of supplies to the top of Quartz Ridge, a rib of rock that soared a thousand feet above camp on the west side of the ice-cascade.

The ridge became more than just a pile of gaunt and barren rock to them. It was the last sizeable outcrop of rock they would see for a month. Beyond was the world of eternal snow and ice where man has a different set of problems, and sometimes has a hard job holding on to his sense of values. Once here in the vast deep-freeze, the body and the mind begin to get rough treatment.

As they walked, for instance, their feet would get numb from the cold of the snow beneath. Yet their faces, not six feet away, would be blistering in a temperature perhaps fifty degrees higher. Snow and ice act as a magnifying reflector, doubling and tripling the burning power of the sun. The thin air never really warms up, but anything directly exposed to the sun's rays will almost bake. At all times, from now on, the climbers' faces were smeared with thick layers of protective cream. Their eyes, too, were guarded, with various types of dark glasses.

MacCarthy's eyes, never very strong, were shielded by two pairs, but the glare was so strong that even then he had frequent pains and headaches. Even when clouds or fog keep out the direct sun, burns and glare can be serious on a mountain. And the climbers were now embarked on a stay of forty-four days on snow and ice.

But they prepared as best they could, and carried twenty-eight loaded packs and one sled to the top of Quartz Ridge. Slowly they began to feel at home. To the mountaineer, things are not quite right until he gets onto steep slopes – slopes where he doesn't have to lean far to rub his nose against the rock or ice. He may mutter as he struggles up them, but this, after all, is the lure of steep and high places that has made him what he is.

The snow route up to the top of the ridge was steep enough for all of them. For considerable stretches, the slope measured forty-five degrees, and they quickly decided to put in a fixed rope handrail for safety as they hauled up the loads. The snow was firm, and the ice-axes, plunged in to the head, held tightly and kept the ropes in place.

Early on the morning of June 3, they abandoned Cascade and with heavy loads began the leap-frog march up King Glacier. Along the west side of the glacier, mountain ramparts soared to 12,000 feet.

Bulging along them were heavy loads of hanging ice, which frequently broke off and fell towards the party. But along the base of the ridge was a huge crevasse, which swallowed up the avalanches and kept the climbers safe. It took them three more days to move the loads to Observation Camp at 10,200 feet.

This was the highest point MacCarthy had reached during his summer reconnaissance the year before. From here on, they were heading where no one had been before. Yet, by the standards of most of the world's mountain ranges, they were not even at the foot of their peak. They still had eighteen miles and almost 10,000 vertical feet to go.

The weather maliciously emphasized their isolation. They pitched the tents in a strong wind that lashed stinging sheets of snow in their faces. That night, it rose to a pitch of extreme violence and several times the climbers struggled to hold up the tent-poles, frightened that their three tiny shelters would be torn away.

Then, suddenly, in the freakish, unpredictable way of big mountains that brew their own weather, the storm ceased. Instead, there was a dead calm and dense fog. The fog swathed and muffled them as they left camp at 9 a.m. next day. This was to be an easy day. Packs weighed only thirty-one pounds, and fastened to each one was a thick bundle of willow wands. This was Andy Taylor's idea, and like all great ideas a very simple one. On big areas of featureless snow and ice, which are common on Alaska's giant glaciers, there is nothing to guide the traveller when the clouds come down. Perspective vanishes; the frowning cliff that towers ahead may turn out to be a foot high. As skiers know to their cost, it is sometimes impossible to tell even whether the ground ahead slopes up or down.

But when a slim willow switch is planted in the snow, without even a break in the planter's stride, the picture changes. The eye has something of recognized stature to focus on. The willows are placed about a hundred feet apart. This way, even in the worst of weather, the last man on the rope can stay with one wand until the leader, casting about in the blizzard, can find the next. Step by hundred-foot step this continues, making safe travel relatively simple in weather that would otherwise be impossible. The thin wands stand up well to storms. Even on icy patches where they cannot be pushed in, three of them tied into a tripod give little for the wind to grasp, and will stand through gales.

They planted them as they went now, even though it was foggy.

16

They knew the line to take, for in the earlier sunshine they had seen King Col and the route of approach. King Col is the flat saddle between the bulk of Logan and the difficult spire of King Peak (16,971 feet).

By 1 p.m. they were four miles above camp, at the base of an ice-fall a thousand feet high. It was a gentle gradient, however, and the hundreds of crevasses were well bridged with firm snow.

But if the gradient was gentle, the weather was not. It became worse as they pushed upwards, and when they went over the top of the ice-fall the blasts became so strong that several of the men were almost skittered into crevasses. They struggled on for another mile in what they called a "mild blizzard, with temperature about zero". At 13,200 feet by their small pocket altimeters they stopped and dumped most of the contents of their packs into the snow. This was about two miles short of the saddle, which they had hoped to reach. As they returned, visibility became even poorer and the wind had wiped out their track, but the wands were easy to follow.

Their success at following the wands decided them to push ahead the next day, June 7, no matter what the weather, and relay more loads to the col. Almost seven hundred pounds of food and fuel were loaded onto the sled, and with all eight either hauling on the lines or pushing on the handles they made four miles to the foot of the ice-fall in four hours. Then they carried the loads to a spot a mile beyond their earlier cache and a mile short of the saddle itself. Terrible winds can howl through high saddles in the mountains, and the site they chose would be sheltered from at least some of them. It was at 14,500 feet. They could hardly wait to dump their loads there and hurry along to the saddle. This was the key: did it lead easily to the base of Mount Logan? Or was it impossible? Nobody had ever seen it.

They stumbled and ran the last few feet to the crest. Then their hope, like their footsteps, staggered at the view. The smooth slopes of the saddle did not connect gently with the upper slopes of their mountain. There was a gap of at least a thousand feet, filled with a chaotic mass of steep and broken ice-blocks. And, just beyond where these finished, the slope curled away out of sight, with no view of the problems beyond.

At the other end of the saddle, however, gentle slopes led to 15,000 feet on King Peak, giving the possibility of a better view of the route.

So, while Lambart took his rope of climbers back to camp to get more loads ready, MacCarthy's rope climbed the shoulder of King Peak. The going was fine when they strapped crampons — long, sharp ice-climbing spikes — to their boots and set off. Soon they were on top of the shoulder, within 2,000 feet of King Peak's summit — yet it would not be climbed until 1952!

From their eagle's eyrie, almost as high as the greatest peak in the Alps, they could see the route, at least to 17,000 feet. It was possible, all right, but even the mountaineer's eye of faith could not grade it as easier than "feasible".

As they sat and studied it, they began to be aware of two phenomena of high altitude. First, the dark-blue sky that shades almost to purple at great heights. It framed the finest view they had on the entire expedition. To the south, the fabulous St. Elias Range hurled its ice-tipped spears into the sky. In every direction swelled the corrugated ranks of mountains, straining to burst the clamp of age-old ice. Beyond was another blue, the greenish-blue of the far and cold Pacific.

The second effect of altitude introduced yet another shade of blue — the blue of melancholy. Several of the climbers had already begun to suffer badly from the effects of high altitude.

This depression can hit at any height above roughly 10,000 feet. It is a feeling for which there is no valid single basis of comparison at sea-level. The air is thin; it contains less oxygen and is under far less atmospheric pressure than our bodies are normally accustomed to. The lack of oxygen is enervating, quickly bringing on the symptoms of exhaustion; but the lack of accustomed nitrogen pressure affects the responses of the brain. One experienced Himalayan mountaineer, describing his feeling of altitude sickness, said he felt like "a sick man climbing in a dream".

Men of strong will find their drive evaporating. Men of gargantuan appetites often want to do nothing more than nibble. And men of great physical strength and perfect condition puff and pant from merely turning over in their sleeping-bags. The brain doesn't work very well, but often, as with drinkers, this seems to bring a feeling that the judgment is better than it is. Usually nobody else in the party notices, as the critical faculties of all are likely to be impaired, even though different people react at varying heights.

At this height of 15,000 feet, however, these men of long experience on big mountains were able to shake off the effects of the altitude for a while. They hurried back down to Observation Camp at 10,200 feet and immediately felt better. On June 8, once more they wearily carried more loads up to Col Camp. Foster, Read, and MacCarthy stayed there, digging several feet down into the snow to provide some sort of wind-break for the tents. Lambart took the others down to continue the exhausting, uninspiring, yet all-important job of bringing up the food.

This night was one of torture for MacCarthy. He tossed and turned for hours in the agony caused by the intense glare in his weakened eyes. Foster, getting into practice for grimmer things to come, treated him as best he could, and they set off at 8 a.m. to see if they could find a way through the worrying ice-fall.

In seven hours they reached 16,500 feet, after five miles of turning and twisting through an incoherent jumble of ice-blocks. Many of these were simply grotesque. Others, in the savage detachment of their birth, had acquired outlines that lent themselves easily to naming, in case a rendezvous should ever be necessary in this wilderness of ice. There was Tent City, the Corkscrew, the Dormer Window, the Stage Coach, and the Friendly Crevasse. The odd adjective for the crevasse, so often the curse and worry of the climber's progress, was simply explained: at one featureless spot where it would be easy to lose the way in fog, the crevasse lip led them directly where they wanted to go. They moved slowly on, hearing always the squeaking and growling and occasional muffled roar that showed the ice-fall was slowly moving, a giant escalator to its own destruction. But none of the blocks toppled near them now, and they chose a camp-site at 17,000 feet, to be known prophetically as Windy Camp.

They were within 3,000 feet of the summit now and were beginning to feel a vague optimism when the weather cleared. But the mountain was simply playing another mean and cunning trick on them: it gave them a clear view of the double peak that topped the ice-mass ahead. This looked suspiciously like the summit and built their hopes too high.

Close as they seemed to be, however, they were once again a little like an advancing army that has to stop its triumphant march to let the supply train catch up. This mountain, though impersonal and non-selective in its fight, was a dangerous enemy, able at any moment to throw a ring of impassable weather around them. At every camp they had to be prepared to wait out a siege of blizzards that might pin them down for a week or more at a time. So all day on June 10 the back-breaking work went on as they hauled supplies to Col Camp, making it a fortress. If they were routed anywhere else on the giant peak, here at 14,200 feet at least was warmth, comparative comfort, and safety.

Early next day it began to snow, which was common for June 11 at this height and so far north. But this was the start of a chain of developments fraught with implications of disaster.

It was almost noon before MacCarthy, Lambart, Foster, and Hall set off with heavy packs towards Windy Camp. The carefully placed footsteps in the snow they had made before, so big a psychological stimulus when men are weary and long for rhythmic guidance to their feet, had vanished under the heavy fall of new snow. They planted willow wands as they navigated the route now established through the clouds, and the careful observation that had gone into the naming of the ice-blocks served them well. Tent City still looked like a city of tents, even if more opulent with its rich re-roofing. Hog Back was still a hog's back, though the hog was sleeker, fat with its surfeit of snow. A little higher, at 15,400 feet, the wallowing became too tough; so they dumped their packs and turned back.

The snow continued to fall monotonously throughout the next two days. They could do little but lie in the tents, joking constantly to hide the fact that although they were vexed and anxious at the delay they were rather glad of the chance to rest.

When all eight set out again at 6.30 a.m. on June 14, the snow had an exasperating crust of ice that was not quite strong enough to support them on snow-shoes. As the weight of their forty-five-pound packs made the crust break, time and again the clumsy snow-shoes would catch on the jagged edge of crust, tripping them up and destroying the rhythm so vital at this altitude. And there was a new danger around them now, the threat that the fresh top layer of snow would peel off with a sibilant hiss and sweep the whole party to destruction. In five and a half hours they climbed 900 feet to the Hog Back – a pleasant half-hour saunter at sea-level. To their forty-five-pound packs they now added the loads dumped here earlier, and moved on, almost imperceptibly. Five trying hours later, they had gained a mere 400 feet, and as they were trying to decide what to do the weather solved their problem: a blizzard hit them with frightening speed. It roared to new heights as they pitched their wildly flapping tents and struggled to crawl through the circular sleeve entrances.

It blew throughout the next day, and the clouds were so thick that it was hard to see the adjoining tents. Early on the sixteenth the wind dropped; so they set out at 6.30 a.m. Twelve battling hours later they reached Windy Camp at almost 17,000 feet, beneath the great southwest wall of Logan. It was a strenuous day, one with which any climbing party could be well satisfied. Instead Foster, Lambart, and MacCarthy left Hall to set up camp and climbed on to prospect the route ahead.

When they came back, just before 8 p.m., the temperature was 27° below zero. That night it went down to 33° below.

Before he settled down for the night, so close to the summit, MacCarthy took a realistic look at the men around him. He was as optimistic as he could reasonably be, but the best entry he could make in his diary was: "Party all in fair shape, but not strong for the work to be done." The night did not improve things. All slept badly, despite the insulation of their sixteen-pound Arctic bedrolls.

When men reach a tired and worn-out state like this, the start of each new day brings a difficult conflict of feeling. The part of the mind that has the body's welfare to worry about puts up a protest. It half prays for fog, snow, a blizzard — anything to give a valid reason for resting longer. The other part, focused by conscience on the job to be done, prods dully but usually irresistibly at the will, striving to convince it that a fine day is most welcome so that they can get on with the hard work.

June 17 started out to be a fine day and, the sleeping-bag skirmish with conscience having been won, they all turned out and began to prepare. MacCarthy summed up their situation with a piece of priceless understatement that would have made any good English stiff upper lip quiver with admiration: "There appearing some need for relaxation from drudgery," he wrote, "all hands went on a reconnaissance in order to determine our exact location on the massif." Many people would have abandoned the whole project right there, for what MacCarthy's statement meant in simple English was: We were too tired to pack camps any farther, and we didn't know where we were anyway.

What the weary troops needed to renew their vigour, MacCarthy decided, was . . . some mountain-climbing. But without heavy packs. The difference between climbing steep slopes with a pack and without one is something that cannot be imagined. It has to be tried. After days of heavy packing, the climber's sense of balance goes to pieces when he suddenly steps out without a load. But it is a quick readjustment and one the climber is pleased to make.

They did it now, and in five hours they had circled to the north side of the mountain and reached a saddle at 18,800 feet that separated two high peaks. Thick fog blocked out the view as they waited in the bitter cold, straining their eyes to see ahead and pick out a route. Where should they turn next? Was one of these double peaks the summit? Which? Or was the highest point even farther away?

Next day, Foster, Read, and MacCarthy climbed back to the saddle again while the others went down for more food. This time, a gale was sweeping the saddle. Lying down in the snow, peering through ice-rimmed eyes over the edge of the saddle, they had a brief glimpse of another double peak about three miles away. As they lay in the snow to avoid being bowled over the edge by the gale, they started to argue. Was that the top? Or was there yet another in this damnable, never-ending ridge?

Only one thing was sure: even a camp at 17,000 feet, where sleep was difficult and the thought of hard work revolting, was not high enough. Windy Camp was too remote from the top for weak and exhausted men to make a safe "dash" to the still invisible summit.

As they turned in that night, the temperature was 32° below zero. At 7 a.m. next day, it was still 25° below, and snowing heavily, but all eight went down for supplies. For an hour in the afternoon, the sun poked holes through the layers of cloud and the temperature began to climb rapidly. At last, it seemed, the weather might help them. An hour later a gale whipped away the last vestige of summer and replaced it in minutes with Arctic winter. This was the worst weather so far, and almost trapped the party between camps. All took it in weary turn to punch foot-holes in the snow, and it was after 9 p.m. when they reached Windy Camp again.

Several fingers were frost-bitten from uncovering them for even the few seconds needed to tighten bootlaces or pack straps. But far more serious was the fact that Morgan's feet, which had been frozen some years before, were now quite badly frost-bitten. This proved to Mac-Carthy that they had reached the limit of usefulness of the rubber shoe-packs they were wearing. These are rubber shoe-pieces with leather boot-uppers attached to them. In the ever-wet going of the lower glaciers, they were a great success. Here, where the snow never melts and the temperature rarely gets as high as freezing-point, the rubber wasn't necessary — and they were far from warm enough. They were big enough for only two pairs of socks. So the party switched to a type of Indian moccasins, dry-tanned and with room enough for up to five pairs of thick socks.

Keeping warm had now become the all-absorbing problem, and the tents were at once the focus and the shield of life. To keep out the crippling cold, each man was now wearing two sets of the heaviest woollen underwear, with long legs and sleeves; windproof canvas trousers; up to three woollen shirts; at least one sweater; and hooded, knee-length parkas of windproof drill cloth. Everybody wore a woollen balaclava helmet and two pairs of wool gloves with windproof over-gauntlets. The tents in which they lived were eight feet square at the base, seven feet high at the one pole, tapering to eighteen inches at the other end. Each weighed ten pounds and slept four men.

Each one had a sewn-in waterproof groundsheet, and on top of this were individual air-mattresses of heavy-gauge rubber. Each of these weighed eight pounds, and a bicycle pump was used to inflate them. Finally came an eiderdown sleeping-bag weighing sixteen pounds. Two of these could be fastened together to make one bag about six feet wide. For twelve days, four of the climbers slept together in one of these. It kept them fairly warm, but they were so cramped that they all slept badly.

Another important aspect of keeping warm at these heights is food. At high altitudes the heartiest eater often becomes finicky. Mountain-eers are generally marked individualists, and many acquire an almost fanatical belief in the value of one food or another. One climber, for instance, almost refused to join this party because he understood no cocoa was being taken. Without it in the diet, he said, the assault would not succeed. Another insisted that jam was the key to success on the mountain. He didn't mind what else was taken provided there was enough jam to permit huge amounts at every meal.

Two of the party fell out on how to cook the bacon. One said vehemently that to be useful it must be burned to a crisp. The other swore it provided most benefit when not cooked but just warmed through.

MacCarthy, who drew up the menu, solved the problem as best he could. He provided far more than he thought the climbers could eat of a variety of meats, butter, cheese, dried eggs and vegetables, powdered milk, and brown sugar. Then for those who wanted to convince themselves they were eating something else, he provided liberal amounts of black pepper, cinnamon, nutmeg, curry, horseradish, and sauces. It seemed to work. Nobody made any real complaints.

But despite the care that had gone into the planning, now at 17,000 feet they were faced with the serious fact that Morgan's feet were badly frost-bitten. He must go down. There was no way to get around it, because cold at high altitude is a vastly different thing from the same temperature at sea-level. Extra warmth and simple treatment would not cure it here.

This is chiefly because the thin air forces the body to adjust in many ways to overcome the lack of oxygen. The same volume of air goes into the lungs with each breath as at sea-level, but it contains much less oxygen. And even that is absorbed less readily by the blood, as it is under less atmospheric pressure.

At sea-level the air is at a pressure of 14.7 pounds per square inch. By 20,000 feet, the pressure has dropped to a mere 6.75 pounds. Researcher Carpé made some simple tests as he went through the wearying ascent that indicate a practical result of the drop in pressure and the lack of oxygen. At sea-level, he found he could hold his breath comfortably for 75 seconds when he was at rest. At 18,500 feet, he could barely hold it for 20 seconds. Up to 14,000 feet, he found that the time he could hold his breath shortened in the same ratio as the air density declined. Above 14,000 feet, the time dropped sharply. Years later, scientists working on Everest and other high peaks found that above 20,000 feet or so, no matter how much the climber eats and drinks, there is actual loss of weight and muscular wasting as the body starts to degenerate.

Animals kept for experiments in an atmosphere corresponding to 20,000 feet showed degenerative changes in the liver and other organs. Nobody has yet had the temerity to keep man in similar conditions as long, but high-altitude physiologists say the same sort of changes would occur in man too.

Even at far lower levels, the body has to make some startling changes. When air pressure is normal, the automatic breathing that we rarely stop to think about is controlled by a part of the brain that reacts to the pressure of nitrogen in the body. When this pressure drops, the automatic control does not work. This may not be too bad when one can consciously think about it, but what happens at night when we drop off to sleep?

Fortunately, the body is marvellously able to switch over to an emergency control system, in which the level of oxygen in the blood controls the automatic breathing. However, the change from one system to another is often a tough one for the body to make. In camp at 13,800 feet, Morgan had suffered a pronounced Cheyne-Stokes respiration – the alarming "death-rattle" heard as a dying man struggles for air. Morgan's system was doing just the same thing – hunting for enough air during the critical change-over period.

Another major adjustment the body makes to get more oxygen into the tissues is a striking increase in the number of red corpuscles in the blood. These are the vehicles for carrying oxygen to the tissues. Increasing the number causes a great thickening of the blood; it becomes sluggish, and cold hands and feet become a perennial problem, despite the best equipment.

The breathing speeds up too. This gives off not only a lot of body heat, but also a great deal of moisture. Measurements indicate that probably three pints of fluid are lost in this way alone in a day's climbing. This, unless it is carefully watched, tends to dehydrate the system even more, and makes the blood even less efficient as a central heating plant for the body.

All these conditions, then, were causing some problems by the time Morgan's feet became affected, and there was no doubt that his decision to go down was wise. For all the problems that had troubled them so far would be redoubled from here on. At the very least, one more camp had to be set up, and even the most efficient body would be balanced on the thin edge of safety.

Henry Hall, so close to one of the finest prizes of his long climbing career, casually did something that showed why he was one of the best known and most respected of United States climbers. He gave up his chance at the peak and offered to take Morgan down to safety. But first, he insisted, he must take the biggest and heaviest pack up to the next camp-site. It didn't matter too much if he wore himself out, he said – he was going downhill from then on. But it would at least lessen by a fraction the odds against the others making it.

He did his last big carry on June 20, when all except Morgan moved up in a storm to a tiny saddle at 18,500 feet. This held for many years the record as the highest regular camp established in North America. On the basis that on a mountain a record altitude figure is worth a dozen adjectives, this has been known ever since as the Camp of Eighteen-Five. Then everybody, travelling light, raced back to Windy Camp. Once more it earned its name. All night long, arctic blasts kept the canvas taut and twanging, and everyone came to feel he was living in an oversized, reverberating drum.

At 10 a.m. the wind eased off long enough for Hall and Morgan to set off down. They shook hands quickly with the remaining six climbers, and wished them well; then, looking frail and puny, they vanished within a rope's length into the swirling clouds of snow. No sooner had they gone than the gale swept back. By 3 p.m. all six had crept into their sleeping-bags, morose and a little anxious about both the prospects above and the pair going down. But there was nothing they could do about either, and they had time to reflect on the futility of man's boast that he "conquers" peaks. When impersonal nature makes a personal issue of it, the strongest climber hasn't a hope of winning. All the great feats of mountaineering have been achieved by skilful men who were ready and waiting for the momentary relaxation of nature's guard that would let them slip in.

So it was now. As suddenly as if somebody had flicked a switch, the wind dropped a few minutes after they crawled into their sleeping-bags. The clouds vanished, and sunshine flooded the slopes. They scurried around packing, and by 10 p.m. were settled in for the night at 18,500 feet. Their two small Brownie tents, smaller and a little lighter than the ones they had used so far, made a brave show of pretending to be safe and comfortable at this near-limit of man's ability.

They found that night and the next morning that the effects of altitude were really beginning to hit everybody. Everything they did was slow and clumsy. Several just lay in their bags and looked with half-glazed eyes at jobs that must be done, thinking dully of ways to avoid them. Even the exertion of getting into the bags, or turning over inside them, set the heart pounding. That night, the temperature was seven degrees below zero – thirty-nine degrees below freezing-point,

Fahrenheit. In fact from June 16 to June 26 the thermometer went above zero only once. So befuddled were they next morning, June 22, that it was 11 a.m. before they could start. Thick-gloved hands fumbled drunkenly with packstraps and snow-shoe bindings, and the main thing that got them going was the collective, not individual, feeling that it just had to be done. All pleasure had long since vanished from the undertaking. This feeling of collective responsibility is one of the major benefits of team psychology. It is nothing unusual for all the members of a climbing rope to feel inside that this is the limit; each feels too tired and dispirited to go on. But nobody will admit it, so they do go on. And what each man thought to himself to be impossible is once again accomplished.

So it was now as they moved away from the Camp of Eighteen-Five. Their route at first took them down from the saddle, skirting the double peak so they would not have to fight for valuable height, only to lose it again on the other side. Yet though they were going down, they made only one and a half miles before deep, soft snow halted them on a plateau at 17,800 feet. This they decided to call Plateau Camp, and with faltering, half-desperate movements they pitched their tents near what was later to be grimly known as Hurricane Hill.

It was fortunate they stopped. As the last man crawled panting through the entrance sleeve, a violent gust of wind raced over the hill, bringing a blizzard that shrieked all night. Hardly anybody could even doze as the night crept slowly on. The splendid peace and tranquillity of the heights that the poets praise was nowhere evident. The wind made so much noise that they rather fancied they were spending the night inside a busy railway tunnel. Much of the time they clutched the vibrating bamboo tent-poles, expecting any moment to see the fabric split and tear apart.

But once again came the seeming surrender of nature that lures men on to try impossible deeds. By 10 a.m. the storm had blown out and the clouds of snow whipped up by its passing had settled down again.

The sun came out − and came nearer to immobilizing the party than even the blizzards. The fearful glare from new white snow was almost intolerable, and the severe pains of approaching snow-blindness shot through MacCarthy's eyes, though he wore two pairs of the darkest snow-goggles made. He was leading the first rope, followed by Carpé, with Foster bringing up the rear. So the rope switched around, to put Foster in front − Foster, whom MacCarthy called "our sheet anchor no matter what the difficulty". Foster seemed to take all types of problems in his stride, and versatility was his forte. He had already been a member of the Legislative Assembly of British Columbia, and, at thirty-five, had been Deputy-Minister of Public Works for the province. He was to become chief of police in Vancouver, and a major-general in the Second World War. In addition to the D.S.O. and two bars he won in the First World War, he also won the Croix de Guerre from France and Belgium – and many years later in England, another colonel was to state that Foster had turned down a nomination for the Victoria Cross, the Commonwealth's highest award for bravery.

Billy Foster led them on the wandering route among crevasses, over a shoulder of ice, and to the base of a steep slope supporting the saddle between two peaks. The Double Peak was clearly visible now, but it was impossible to say which of the summits was the higher.

A brief rest here, and MacCarthy tenaciously took back the lead. During the 1924 reconnaissance he had tried vainly to decide which of these giant twin peaks was the summit. At various times he and his binoculars had awarded the title to each. Now he set off up the nearest one, with the feeling that this was probably not the summit, but that the only way to find out was to go up it.

The slope was now steeper than anything they had met so far on the mountain. Two weak men would find it almost impossible to hold a third who slipped. But their eight-pointed crampons bit firmly into the icy crust. All they had to do was keep placing each foot in turn in front of, and a little above, the other.

This simple-sounding feat was excellently described almost thirty years later when Wilfred Noyce was at 21,000 feet on Mount Everest. He wrote:

> Heart aches,
> Lungs pant,
> The dry air
> Sorry, scant.
> Legs lift
> and why at all.
> Loose drift
> Heavy fall.
> Prod the snow
> It's easiest way;
> A flat step
> is holiday.

At 4.20 p.m., with the sun glaring from an unclouded sky, all six reached the top. As they tramped slowly onto the summit the first place everybody looked was to the south-east. There the companion dome glittered wickedly two miles away. There was a painful silence as they looked, for what they felt was far too deep for mere curses. The distant mound was obviously higher than the one on which they stood. Hoping to prove that his eyes were wrong, surveyor Lambart pulled with freezing fingers the surveying level from his pack. The obvious was formally confirmed; they still had another mountain to climb. And the gulf between was almost 1,000 feet deep.

MacCarthy, Foster, and Carpé set off directly towards the exasperating summit. Lambart, Read, and Taylor, gambling that this peak was their goal, had left most of their equipment at the base of it. They would have gone back for it anyway, but they particularly wanted the last few willow-wands that were tied to their packs. Half an hour later, they were all together once more in a saddle beneath what they hoped was their final trial, the ultimate apex of Canada.

The pitiful pace slowed even more. In this region of almost perpetual wind, the powdered snow could not stay for long. Brittle, shining ice gleamed in the open, and as they manoeuvred around these patches they had to cut almost two hundred steps in the crusted snow. The slope was frighteningly steep to tackle at this height – in several places it was about sixty degrees. Every movement had to be safeguarded carefully, by ramming the ice-axe as far down into the snow as possible and then paying the rope out slowly around it. It was Carpé's job to safeguard the leader, but MacCarthy knew that if he fell he could expect little except psychological help from the rope. Carpé was exhausted, and had to be helped to move on the final stretch. But finally, while MacCarthy was cutting steps like an automaton, with no conscious thought to guide his axe, his head came level with the top of the ridge. A hundred yards away, at the top of a gentle rise, stood the summit.

It was here, so close to victory, that MacCarthy thought for a moment he had gone mad. For days the altitude and hard work had made them all light-headed, with delusions that they were hopping through time and space, like giants in seven-league boots performing prodigious feats. Now into MacCarthy's tired and disbelieving brain flashed the picture of a giant's head, framed in a vivid, circular rainbow.

"Now I was possibly seeing the unreal," he wrote, "perhaps one of nature's brilliant hoops through which I must jump when legs and feet felt like lead after their long ordeal." It was a relief to his brain when Carpé, the scientist, said matter-of-factly that it was a "Brocken spectre with a halo". When the sun's rays coincide with the direction in which the climber is looking, the shadow of his head is sometimes projected onto the outside edge of a cloud to form the spectre. The rainbow halo comes from light hitting the liquid droplets in the air which stay un-frozen even at the temperature of near zero. MacCarthy had never seen either before.

A few more minutes took them to the top, crampons crunching with a squeak into the hard snow of the knife-edged summit ridge. It was 8 p.m. The summit was a thirty-foot pinnacle of ice, just big enough for the six of them to stand on. The sides dropped thousands of feet to remote untrodden glaciers below.

MacCarthy recorded the scene this way: "We veritably seemed to be standing on top of the world, with King Peak and many others that had looked like insurmountable heights now lying below us, and appearing in the vast sea of foam as mere specks of flotsam. This effect, it seemed to me, was out of all proportion to the variation in altitude. Or is it with altitude as with gravitation, radiation and hunger, in proportion to the square of the distance from the object?

"As the most ravenous member of the party, perhaps, described it, here below us was a huge layer cake with its nuts showing through the frosting; a veritable sea of white expanse with myriads of islands, and all thousands of feet below."

But even as they revelled in the view — and the faculty of observa-tion, curiously, remains virtually undulled as altitude saps the other senses — clouds began bubbling and boiling up in the direction of Mount St. Elias, a cauldron filled with storm and trouble. As they stood numbly on the summit, burying in the snow a brass tube with their names and the date, and munching cheese, chocolate, and dried fruits, they shook hands all round.

"We were foolishly happy in the success of our venture," said Cap-tain MacCarthy, "and we thought that our troubles were at an end."

Lambart was the first to leave the summit, with Taylor and Read on his rope. It was almost 8.30 p.m., and as Carpé, Foster, and Mac-

Carthy left a few seconds later it was obvious that they were in for a dangerous race with the weather. In a few short minutes, it was equally obvious that they had lost it. Thick cloud enveloped them, and they had trouble following even the big steps they had hacked out on the way up the final steep slopes. Where the going flattened out between this and the other Double Peak, there were no steps to follow. The sharp crampons had left no trail in the hard crust – and the last of the willow-wands was a mile away, where the supply had run out.

The wind rose, and began to punch the reeling party in shattering gusts that all but knocked them flat. Flying snow in the air blended with the snow on the surface to produce that phenomenon so much feared by Arctic travellers: the "white-out". In this condition it is impossible to tell direction, or even which way the ground slopes. Now they were wandering aimlessly. Five hours after they left the summit, at 1.30 a.m., they were still at the 19,000-foot level, and hopelessly lost. They had no choice but the one that many experienced climbers would have considered near-certain death – to spend the night huddled in holes in the snow.

Moving like sick, apathetic shadows of the men they had been two weeks before, they began pecking out holes with the narrow points and adzes of their ice-axes. Snow-shoes served, though not too well, as shovels, but the energy that is the primary tool for digging reasonable shelters just was not there. They had reached the penultimate plateau of exhaustion, a plateau sloping gently down towards oblivion, where the body's strength has gone and only the spur of the mind is left.

This in itself, though usually on a less epic scale, is part of the fascination of mountaineering: the realization that each difficult climb can take you far beyond the physical limits of ordinary life, and that each worth-while success may bring a new boundary of self-realization to cross. It is the dogged crossing of this boundary that gives rise to all the great feats of adventure.

There was little thought of adventure in their minds as they chipped away at their task. There was little, if any, conscious thought that they must do this to survive. The holes they made were so poor and inadequate that if they had been forced to put sled-dogs in them, the climbers would have felt sorry for the dogs. "They were pitiful evidences of the weakened state of our party," wrote the leader. Carpé still had the will-power to check the temperature: it was −12° F., and dropping quickly. But when the thermometer fell into the snow, he didn't have the energy to scrabble for it, and it soon vanished in a soft drift. Exhaustion fought with the fear of freezing to death, and won in fitful snatches. But wild attacks of shivering and frightening nightmares woke them time and time again. Much to their surprise, all lived to see the dawn, which was indicated merely by an infinitesimal lightening of the dark shades of gloomy grey. Still they could see nothing in the whirling snow.

Writing of this grim situation, MacCarthy once more outdid himself in understatement. He wrote: "A further period under such trying conditions might have reduced some of our members to a helpless state. So at noon I called all hands and ordered a start with Andy leading."

Andy Taylor, who lived in the north and was accustomed to the bitter cold of Arctic winter, was probably less affected by the long exposure than any of the others. He was ready to go at once. But the leader and Foster, who was hero-worshipped by the men he had led into dangerous battles, found it was one thing to order — even in a weak and faltering shout — and quite another to get people to obey, even when the order was meant to save their lives. It was another two hours before the rest of the party could be pried from the near-death stupor they had sunk into in the holes that so nearly became their tombs.

The great need now was action — exercise to start the frigid blood pumping through their stiff, sore bodies. But almost as great was the need for caution. One false move in the deceptive, dangerous, flat light could put them over the brink of an ice-cliff. MacCarthy took the leader's place for descent — at the end. Like the captain of a sinking ship, the leader comes last, to make sure everybody else is safe. He is the anchor man, ready and competent to check any slips that he sees developing among the men on the rope below him. The most skilled man comes down last on the rope, too, because he is the only one who will have to descend without a rope from above.

MacCarthy was barely able to see the others on the rope, and he marvelled, in a detached sort of way, at the exaggerated drunken swaying of his companions. Suddenly, the caution drummed into him by years of imminent danger in the mountains snapped his mind back into focus. A faint black streak, hardly visible, appeared through the mist a few feet to his right. Cautiously he edged nearer to investigate it, and found to his horror a cliff dropping off into the bottomless shroud of space.

"I hastened forward to give Andy warning, but it was too late," he wrote. "In a moment he disappeared from sight, with the rope left taut in Read's hands." MacCarthy hurried up to help Read take the strain on the rope, and moved carefully to the edge of the precipice, afraid of what he might see when he looked down. Thirty feet below, motionless and half buried in the snow, was Taylor. MacCarthy called urgently to him, but he did not move. MacCarthy called again, his voice pitched higher now in desperation. And this time Taylor answered. He was unhurt, but temporarily paralysed by having his breath knocked out as he landed.

A few feet farther along, the cliff curved down to a low point close to the level where Taylor had landed. The five climbers moved along to this, and after Taylor had a few minutes to get his breath back they were able to haul him back to safety.

MacCarthy was so relieved to have escaped disaster that he found the energy to pull Taylor's leg about it. It was frightfully bad form, he said, for Taylor to have left the other members of his rope without giving them proper warning. It raised a laugh, but as a joke it backfired.

A few minutes later MacCarthy tumbled over an unseen ice-cliff and dropped fifteen feet before Carpé and Foster held him with a rib-crushing check on the rope.

Despite an ordeal that would have destroyed lesser parties, they still pushed slowly on. And finally they had a stroke of luck — the kind that comes only to top-flight men of long experience. Nobody really knew where they were going, but Taylor, with nothing but instinct to guide him in the white-out, kept heading obstinately to where he insisted they would find the last willow-wand. They found it, with Read's sharp eyes spotting it first. Just the sight of a slender stick they had cut from a wilderness bush was enough to send new strength into their legs, proof enough of the mind's control of the body's limits.

MacCarthy summed it up this way: "The reaction was the same as I once felt when struggling in a hopeless surf that rapidly carried me seaward, with combers strangling every effort I made to catch breath. I finally gave up, let go — and my feet touched the bottom. In an instant I had the strength of a giant, and incautiously jumped to my feet, only to have them swept from under me again. But deliverance was there, and I did not say good-bye to this world that day."

He didn't say good-bye to the world on this day of trial by ice on the mountain either — in fact he lived to be eighty, and died in Annapolis, Maryland, in 1956. But neither did he say good-bye to the terrors of being lost high on Mount Logan.

Taylor, Read, and Lambart followed the wands to Plateau Camp, the two flimsy tents at 17,800 feet. Taylor would hold onto one wand while Read, at the other end of the rope, would pass by him and look for the next wand, a hundred feet away in the driving blizzard. Then Read would hold on to this one while Taylor passed him.

But MacCarthy, Foster, and Carpé, the most experienced climbers of them all, stopped for a moment to tighten a packstrap. They lost touch with the other rope in a few seconds, became confused by the storm, and headed on, hoping to pick up the willow-wand trail again. They tramped slowly for an hour, and as they went something niggled at the methodical mind of Carpé. At first his weary brain just sensed that something was wrong, although it was too tired to puzzle it out. Suddenly he realized: the rise of the slope was on their right now, instead of on their left as it had been before. They all realized instantly what had happened. In their brief pause the fury of the storm had made them turn completely around and they were now heading back towards the peak — away from safety. With spirits too drained for emotion, they turned around, and plodded back for another hour. By now, however, the grey of night was blending with the whirling clouds, and they were forced to stop until daylight.

It was a night of delirious rambling, of hallucinations and moments of cold sanity when they "knew" they would never escape a second time.

"High cliffs of ice would seem to rise up before us to block our way," MacCarthy wrote, "and yet we never encountered them. Barns and shelters would suddenly appear that we knew could not exist, for otherwise one's companions would surely suggest taking refuge in them."

It was so cold that they abandoned their idea of staying in one place until they could see properly. They trudged on automatically through the night, twice routinely scraping out feeble shelters for naps that never lasted long enough to overcome their shivering.

34

With dawn, however, came visibility. With it, the pressing problems vanished; they could see their way to Plateau Camp and by 5 a.m. they were wolfing chicken for breakfast after a harrowing thirty-four hours. By 6 a.m. they were asleep. They awoke at 4 p.m., and stayed awake just long enough for another meal; then went back to sleep to build up strength for the trip out. It was no downhill stroll, as they first had to climb to the Camp of Eighteen-Five, a difficult task in their present condition.

Now, with the lash of imminent death no longer curling around their shoulders, reaction to their terrible ordeal began to hit all the climbers. They were up by 6 a.m. on June 26, but even though "mares' tails" in the sky warned them that more storms were on the way, it took five hours to get ready to move off. Even then, they left the tents, mattresses, clothing, and spare food behind. Taylor's rope went first, snowshoeing along the line of looming willow-wands. The going was good, rhythm began returning to their weary legs, and spirits improved.

Then they reached a steep, rounded snow dome where the winds had compressed the snow to a hard crust. It was impossible to get up it on cumbersome snow-shoes, so they began to change to their sole-fitting crampons.

As they did so, the weather launched its most vicious attack yet. A hurricane hit them, and the temperature plummeted. The normally simple task of tying the long tapes of the crampons became almost impossible. The strings rapidly became almost unmanageable bars of ice. Bare hands were needed to manipulate them in the freezing wind.

Everybody suffered frost-bite in the fingers as the painful but imperative task of tying the crampons went slowly on. Most of the party had touches of frost-bite in their feet too, and several were temporarily blind from the combination of glare and icy particles hurled horizontally into their faces. The agony of Hurricane Hill was unanimously voted the most terrifying experience so far, even by those who survived the two nights out near the summit.

Somehow they managed to finish the job and push on. By 3 p.m. they were at the site of the Camp of Eighteen-Five, where a small granite rib split the fury of the storm and gave them some shelter. Now the way out was all downhill — and the retreat gave the first signs of turning into a rout. Already they had abandoned two tents at Plateau Camp, and had no safeguard in case of a high-level accident. They struggled on to Windy Camp (16,700 feet), where there was another tent and a cache of supplies. This too they abandoned, with only one thought in their cold-dimmed brains: "Get down before it is too late." The six strong men could hardly muster the strength to pull the shoe-packs from a corner of the partly-collapsed tent; then on they went again.

Once more, they were back in thick fog and fast-flying snow; but this time the thin green wands stood out like oak trees. New avalanches of disintegrating ice had blotted out parts of their route through the ice-fall, but as they passed the last unstable pinnacles of ice they could see three tents half-buried in the snow at Col Camp (14,500 feet). Getting to them was still a major task, however. Avalanche danger was now extreme, with masses of newly-fallen snow poised to slide. The urge was strong to rush straight down to camp and the safe comfort it represented. Instead, they forced themselves to be slow and desperately careful. An accident here could turn triumph to disaster just as surely as one at the summit 5,000 feet above. And this was the likely place for an accident to happen: most mountaineering accidents happen not in the difficult places where mind and muscle are at top pitch, but on the way down, in the anti-climax after success.

It was 1.30 a.m. when they reached camp, and they stayed thirty-six hours, although the altitude was high for sick, bone-weary men. At this camp, Foster showed the unselfish spirit that had earned him the devotion of his men in the war. While the others lay exhausted in their sleeping-bags, he moved methodically around with the first-aid kit. All Lambart's toes were badly frozen, and so were several of Carpé's. The first joints on all MacCarthy's fingers and thumbs were already turning black. Everybody in the party needed some sort of treatment. Then, when he had fixed up the others as best he could, Billy Foster began to look after the eleven small patches of frost-bite that had nipped his own body.

When the body has taken so much punishment, it is hard for even the most active mind to persuade it to leave any level of comfort, no matter how slight. Even the thought of a well-stocked camp at Cas-cade, at an elevation where a man would feel like a whole man again, was barely able to move them. When finally they did move, on June 28, they once more abandoned almost everything and pushed on down. Andy Taylor went first. He went unroped, despite the ever-present danger of vanishing into a crevasse, and dragged behind him his pack, wrapped in a canvas sheet. This gouged a deep, smooth trench in the soft snow and made it easier for the others to get down. It was a brave and dangerous performance by Taylor, and the fact that he volunteered to do it at all indicates how tired and sick his companions must have seemed to him.

By 9 p.m. they were back at Quartz Ridge, at the top of the last 1,000-foot snow slope above Cascade advanced base camp. On June 2, they had made this descent in fifteen minutes. Now it took them twelve times as long – three hours. They crawled through the tent-sleeves just after midnight, and MacCarthy noted in his diary: "Tents in bad shape, but I in worse condition." But no matter how bad it was, they were at least down to 7,800 feet, where men can breathe in comfort, turn over in bed without getting palpitations, and rest without frightening worries about tomorrow.

For two days they rested here while Foster took ceaseless care of the sick. They set off again on July 1. The glaciers were fast losing their deep mantle of winter snow to the summer sun, and the travel was wet and slow. It was dangerous, too, as the constant melting rotted the firm layers of snow that had bridged the deep crevasses on the journey in. So they began to travel at night. At this elevation, the snow still froze at night, strengthening the crevasse bridges, and generally making the surface easier for pulling the two heavy sledges.

Now the worry of high, stormbound camps had gone, and was replaced by a restless drive to get home. Even the discovery that the first big food-cache had been destroyed by bears did not bother them. They rested a few hours near the ruins, and pushed on. On July 4, they stepped off the ice of Chitina Glacier onto vegetation that looked startlingly green and lush to eyes that had seen only ice and snow for forty-four days. Bears had demolished the food-cache here too, but on July 6 they reached the comfort of Hubrick's Camp.

It had taken tremendous endurance to walk so far on frost-bitten feet, but here Lambart, Carpé, and Read decided their feet were so bad they couldn't possibly walk any farther. Raw flesh was visible where the dead surface tissues had sloughed off. Yet the base at the village of McCarthy was still eighty miles away.

In desperation, they decided to try to float down the turbulent Chitina River system on home-made rafts. For several days they worked, building two small rafts that were solemnly christened Logan and Loganette. They looked frail, inadequate things to carry six lives through the rapid, twisting channels of the Chitina. Each was made of six small logs, lashed together, with a small platform on which the baggage could be carried high out of the water.

Early on the afternoon of July 11 they set off. Taylor, Read, and Lambart were riding on Logan, and MacCarthy, Carpé, and Foster on Loganette. After a hair-raising ride of more than fifty miles, Taylor's craft landed that night on a beach at the nearest point to the village of McCarthy. This still left them a thirty-mile walk across rough country to safety. Lambart's feet were far worse than anybody else's, yet he managed the trek next day without food and practically unaided.

The three men on Loganette, who had been forced to spend the second night out near the summit, ran out of luck here too. Only eighteen miles from their starting-point, they met disaster, and barely escaped alive. In one particularly rough stretch of river their raft turned completely over, pitching all three into the glacial water. They managed to grab the raft and paddle their way to shore, but all their camping and cooking equipment was lost. There were still seventy miles to walk, and all they had was a few scraps of emergency rations.

On their pain-wracked feet, the seventy miles took them four days. Just as they reached the village on July 15, they met a party led by Taylor that was setting out to search the bars of the Chitina for their bodies.

The details of their tremendous feat thrilled the mountaineering world – and obviously frightened it a little too, for it was twenty-five years before anybody even attempted the mountain again.

Nightmare Moulded in Rock

MOUNT WADDINGTON

Map on page vi

The tiny plane carrying Sir Edmund Hillary of Everest banked steeply, flew right at the face of Canada's highest mountain outside the Yukon-Alaska border area, and then sped like an arrow between its twin summit spires.

Seconds later we flew back over the 13,177-foot summit of Mount Waddington and Hillary put his finger on what to him was one of the most puzzling problems in modern mountaineering. "It's a wonderful peak," he said, "one of the finest I have ever seen. But why have no Canadians climbed it yet?"

It was December 5, 1955, and he asked the question when he took time out to fly to Waddington with us in a Pacific Western Airlines Beaver. At the time, he was making a brief stop-over in Vancouver on his way to the Antarctic to prepare for his amazing trip to the South Pole.

Hillary had read several accounts of attempts to climb Mount Waddington, including the book *The Unknown Mountain* by the late Don Munday, who, with his wife, knew the peak better than anybody else in the world. Mrs. Munday was with us as we flew the 175 miles north-west from Vancouver, and, as she rapidly named the Coast Range peaks stretching up towards us, Sir Edmund began to get a better idea of the problem.

Thousands of square miles of snow and ice and steep-walled fiords reached out in all directions. A pale sheen of thin December sunshine flickered like a frozen flame over the thick white coat of alpine winter. Hundreds of peaks on which nobody had yet set foot marched in wild and ragged ranks from the glacial green of the inlets. Nowhere a road, or a mine, or a home. Nothing but the frozen stillness of an ice-bound world apart.

Waddington itself towers over 400 square miles of almost Arctic desolation, in which at the high levels there is not a single tree to offset the frightening grandeur of the glacier ice and splintered spires of rock.

After the first assaults of winter, the mountain floated now like a pointed cloud of feathery ice, high above the rest of the countless peaks. We circled closer and closer in tightly-turned orbits around it until Sir Edmund said, "If I'd brought my ice-axe along, I could almost cut steps up it from here." The rest of us felt that our superb pilot, Dan McIvor, was trying to do the job for him with the wing-tips, so close did they come to the festooned ice on the precipices. Not an inch of rock showed through the frieze of ice.

Then Captain McIvor said, "Now we'll give you a real thrill." Over went the wing, down slid the nose, and it seemed that we were hurtling right at the precipice of the main tower. To the left was the north-west peak, only sixty feet lower than the summit tower. Mrs. Munday, the first person to climb this north-west peak, was so excited she could hardly sit in her seat. Sir Edmund, red-faced with eagerness, was lowering his window, poking his camera towards the sub-zero slipstream. Then we were zooming through the ice-bound cleft, which looked barely wide enough for an eagle's wings.

As we pulled up on the other side, photographer Villy Svarre, born in the low, flat land of Denmark, said, "You teach me how to climb mountains, and I'll come back to try to climb this one."

McIvor turned and banked. Below us, too close, was the spot where an American climber died on Mount Serra in 1947. Straighten up. Nose down. Throttle back. We were almost hanging in the thin, still air of 14,000 feet. Then down to the gap we glided again. No man had stood here yet, though many had tried. The years of history dropped away as quickly as the plunging cliffs below us . . . .

Waddington's history is not long, but what it lacks in length it makes up in glamour and excitement. Sixteen expeditions attacked it before it fell, and it was the most sought-after prize in North American mountaineering. Newspapers in Vancouver, British Columbia, labelled it a "killer peak" and "absolutely impregnable". *The Times* of London carried learned articles on it, and the *Illustrated London News* ran many pictures and articles on "Unclimbed and Unclimbable Mt. Mystery".

It came by its "Mount Mystery" title honestly. The peak is the highest one wholly in British Columbia, and easily Canada's highest outside the Yukon-Alaska border area. It is only twenty-four miles from tidewater, and its chief glacier comes down to within 1,000 feet of sea-level at the head of Knight Inlet. For many years there had been reports from ships out at sea of a giant peak floating above the clouds. But the position was never pinpointed accurately, and nobody really considered it as a rival to Mount Robson, 12,972 feet, the highest mountain in the Canadian Rockies, which is also in British Columbia.

Even in 1925, the chief geographer of British Columbia wrote: "Apart from the lofty section at the northern limits of B.C. . . . there are no known peaks as high as some of those of the Rocky Mountains." The previous summer, however, a Vancouver geologist, Dr. Victor Dolmage, had been making a survey of the Chilko Lake area, about fifty miles east of Waddington. In 1925 he reported ". . . one exceptional peak [which], judging by instrumental observations on it from several triangulation stations, is over 13,000 feet."

For years his report was politely ridiculed. Hardly anybody put any faith in the possibility that the tangled, 1,000-mile Coast Range held a higher peak than Robson. Fortunately, however, two people believed it — Mr. and Mrs. Don Munday, who had always cherished the hope that the Coast Range's unexplored wilderness would contain some giant peaks. In June 1925 they climbed Mount Arrowsmith (5,962 feet), the dominant peak on the southern half of Vancouver Island, and a magnificent spot from which to explore with the eye the convolutions of the Coast Range.

41

After a severe snow-storm, the weather was exceptionally clear as they studied the mountain walls rising from the moat of Georgia Strait — so clear that 150 miles north they "discovered amid the clouds the black bulk of a massive mountain too rugged to be whitened by the storm, and apparently the monarch of its district. It was readily picked out with the naked eye." This, they felt sure, was Dolmage's giant peak. Finding it from the ground, however, was a different problem, as the maps of the area consisted mainly of grid lines separated by stern white space.

That September, they sailed north to look for their mountain. They headed up Bute Inlet, which carves a spectacular trench through the mountains for forty miles and is one of a group of inlets that, a surveyor wrote, "rival in their magnificence all examples of the fiord type in the world". The party climbed Mount Rodney, which soars almost 8,000 feet sheer out of the inlet. It proved a fine viewing-point, and they quickly spotted the mountain they had seen from Arrowsmith. But it was the wrong one — and now for the first time they saw the peak they were to spend so much of their lives exploring and trying to climb.

Don Munday wrote: "Mt. Massive, the mountain that had lured us forth, was still 30 miles away to the north. Its form strongly suggests that it is volcanic in character. But in spite of being fully 10,000 feet in height, it was now seen to be completely outranked in altitude by a lofty range to the west. These greater peaks rose in orderly succession westward, culminating in a giant of unchallenged supremacy."

As the great peak was so close to tidewater, Munday optimistically felt, despite his knowledge of Coast Range travel, that the trip to it up the Homathko River "did not appear unduly formidable at first sight".

He could have learned much from the experience of an earlier traveller, whose efforts to get through the same river valley cost him heartbreak and bankruptcy, and started a minor Indian war. This man was Alfred Waddington, who dreamed of building a railway through here, and after whom the mountain was eventually named. In 1863, Waddington had to build forty bridges to travel thirty-three miles along the turbulent Homathko. From every side-valley glacier-fed streams rush in, so swift and violent that once the water comes above the knees of a wading man he cannot stand up. And the matted jungle of bush is so thick that a strong party can hack its way through only a mile or two a day in the worst places.

Alfred Waddington, an English-born industrialist running one of his mother's cotton mills in France, developed wanderlust in his forties, and sailed to Brazil and California. He was fifty-seven when he arrived in British Columbia in 1858, the year of the province's formal birth. At this time, the Cariboo sand-bars on the Fraser River were yielding rich quantities of gold dust, and the region was flourishing as miners flocked there from all around the world.

Reaching the bars, however, was a tremendous undertaking, and the terrible journey up the Fraser and through its canyons took a heavy toll of life. Waddington received permission to seek a shorter land route from the coast to the gold-workings, and in 1863 he formed a syndicate to finance the cutting through of a preliminary road from the head of Bute Inlet via the Homathko River.

By April 1864, work was well under way in the sombre, claustrophobic canyons of the Homathko. So were the elements of a swift and tragic end to his plans. The Chilcotin Indians, who occupied the land at the head of the river, bitterly resented the ways of some of the early white traders. Their tribe had been ravaged by smallpox, which some reports said was spread by traders who plundered Indian graves to recover infected blankets which they then sold back to the Indians.

One spring morning things came to an explosive head. Three Indians asked road-gang ferryman Timothy Smith for food. He refused, so they killed him. Then they departed, whooping, to collect their friends for a murderous debauch. Near a trail camp a dozen miles away at Murderers' Bar they quietened down. At midnight they crept silently to a big tent, slashed the tent ropes, and stabbed twelve struggling road-makers to death through the canvas. Nineteen people were killed by the end of the massacre, which led to the "Chilcotin War". A punitive expedition, which included newly-appointed Governor Seymour, managed to calm the uprising, and in September of the following year five of the murderers were hanged after a trial at the Cariboo town of Quesnel.

Waddington tried to keep his dream alive, though nearly bankrupted by the disaster. In 1871 he sold his plans for a transcontinental railway through the Homathko to the federal government. He had been one of the strongest advocates of a transcontinental railway for Canada, and often lectured about it in England. But when it was built fifteen years later, the railway used the Fraser Canyon, far to the south.

On his many trips through the Homathko Valley, Waddington became very familiar with the area. But it is unlikely that he ever saw the peak that now carries his name. Mount Waddington appears from the valley in only one or two places, and then as a quite insignificant rock spire mixed up in a tangle of many others. On the project Waddington employed an artist, Frederick Whymper, whose celebrated English brother Edward Whymper was in 1863 making his sixth vain attempt to climb the Matterhorn. (Edward, too, was an artist, who had never climbed a mountain in his life until a publisher sent him on a sketching tour of the Alps.)

Frederick Whymper made sketches of the peaks rising in breathtaking bounds right from the valley floor. Later surveyors took the outline of one of these peaks, and inferred that this was the giant peak. In fact, as Don Munday proved later, it was a bold rock peak little more than 9,000 feet high. Today it is known as Whymper Dome.

In 1926, the Mundays set out for their Mystery Mountain, and discovered for themselves the terrors of travelling the Homathko. Their party included Thomas Ingram, A. E. Agur, R. C. Johnson, and Munday's brother Bert. When they came back, Munday wrote of the Homathko: "It is a wild river in a wild land. It is from 300 to 1,000 feet wide, a silt-burdened torrent forever gouging new channels through magnificent timber, forever filling old channels with sand and driftwood to encourage growth of fresh victims for its insatiate maw.

"We who have lain awake nights beside its grey flood and held our breath as we listened to the reverberant splintering of giant trees in the irresistible river current respect the fury of the Homathko.

"Through 'bear gardens' of strongly interlaced elderberry, salmonberry, kinnie-kinnie and devil's club 10 and 12 feet high we hacked our trails, returning sometimes to find them completely washed away."

The valley was overrun with bears, including grizzlies, and with wolves and cougars, or mountain lions. There was nothing left of Waddington's trail, so they started out by using a canoe. It became holed and battered so badly that they soon abandoned it, and began relaying heavy packs through the bush. By the time they had reached Coula Glacier, twenty-five miles up-river, the party had covered more than a hundred miles on their relays.

The assault petered out at 10,000 feet, when they were only at the foot of Spearmen Peak, a jagged ridge of pinnacles south-east of the main summit. But at least they finally had a good look at their moun-

44

tain. And what they saw was, to say the least, impressive. Don Munday wrote: "There is much that is fantastic – granite crags weirdly caricaturing man and beast; one contemptuous peak has a completely overhanging summit to prevent climbing; half the ruinous side of another is seemingly propped by a slender lone pillar.

"Even the Mystery Mountain has a freakish twist to its symmetrical majesty of form. Its basic black rock seems to have utterly shattered several times, the whole ruin being repaired with intrusions of varicolored rock so that the towering precipices now bear a tracery so wild and uncanny that they might seem prison walls on which tortured fallen spirits had recorded their sufferings.

"Little imagination is needed to liken the stupendous final upthrust of the peak to some prehistoric monster rearing a leering, watchful head high above the utter desolation of rock and ice and snow."

The trip that earned them this view kept them climbing for thirty-two hours, and they were continually roped together for twenty-four hours. As they walked along the snow in the moonlight on the way back to camp, they were so tired that one of them could see only endless sand-bars and log-jams instead of snow. Another kept dodging the branches of non-existent trees, and mistaking shadows of the man ahead for patches of heather on which he might rest.

But when normality came back, they agreed on one thing: Mystery Mountain itself was no mirage, but theirs was not the best way to reach it.

In 1927, the Mundays went back, this time with Mrs. Munday's sister, Mrs. Betty McCallum. This time they went to the head of Knight Inlet, the next one north of Bute, and even wilder and more majestic. Only six miles away from the inlet, and a little over 500 feet above sea-level, they came to the snout of the Franklin Glacier. It is more than twenty miles long, and with the vast ice-field at its head was bigger, Munday estimated, than the entire Columbia Icefield, the largest in the Canadian Rockies.

Travel on the glacier was difficult. At places where subsidiary glaciers joined the main slow-motion flow, pressure ridges like waves in a river piled up chaotic, tumbling walls thirty feet high. Lacework patterns of deep and rumbling crevasses barred the way, and caused wearying problems as the climbers carried loads of up to seventy-five pounds. Finally, they reached an altitude of 11,000 feet on the south-west ridge. At this point, the route was blocked by towers of crumbling rock, which made further attempts there far too dangerous to be worth even considering. Later, they were to see one of these towers crumble, and spray sudden destruction on the route they had taken that day.

They returned to camp just in time to be stormbound in their tent for seven days. As soon as the weather improved, they attacked the mountain by the south-east face. It looked reasonable as a route – but by the time they reached 10,500 feet they realized that the reasonable route could be murderous. The heat of the day loosened snow and rocks above them, which fell with a nerve-wracking regularity.

Both women were badly bruised and Mrs. Munday's hair was matted with blood from a head injury. Mrs. McCallum escaped a similar injury only because Mrs. Munday, with a lightning reflex, flashed out an arm to save her sister's head from a falling rock. The place they reached as a result of all this effort and danger was a dead end. To have gone farther, Munday decided, "would have violated the rudimentary principles of good climbing". After twenty-seven hours on this route, they gave up – but not for long.

After a few hours' sleep, they set off for the other end of the mountain, to Fury Gap, which is about 8,700 feet high and is the only real break for miles in the well-defined crest of the Coast Range. The great West Ridge of Waddington starts here and makes its saw-toothed journey to the twin peaks of the summit. On this ridge are ten distinct summits, all over 10,000 feet high. On this fierce-looking crest, Mrs. Munday felt, lay the best route to the top.

They left their bivouac camp at 5 a.m., and began the serrated journey upward. At several points, the subsidiary peaks up which they climbed were found to be overhanging on the far sides, causing difficult problems as they fought their way along. They lunched at 11,500 feet, their highest level on the mountain so far, and, as they ate, the rocks beneath their feet began to quiver and grumble. While they looked on in awe, a section of the south-west ridge collapsed, near where they had turned back on their first attempt a few days before. Thousands of tons of rotten rock swept down like a tidal wave of dirty foam, and obliterated the route through the snow that they had taken to start the climb up the ridge.

On they went, and came to the foot of the 1,500-foot snow and ice slope leading to the north-west peak. The top had now disappeared in an ominous layer of cloud, and the route ahead was strewn with shattered blocks of ice that had tumbled from the unseen heights above. By 7 p.m. they were at the bottom of a bare-ice slope, only 400 feet from the top, when snow-clouds swirled thick around them, warning of a dangerous storm approaching. It took more courage, Munday said later, to make the right decision when they were so close to the peak than to risk everything on a "heroic" decision to press on to the top. He made the right decision – if climbing is to remain a sport instead of a foolhardy gamble – and they turned and dashed for safety.

The climb that had been very hard in daylight was frightening in a night storm, and it was almost midnight before they could make their way off the summit ice-cap. As they were descending a mountain they later called Fireworks Peak, which towers 1,800 feet above Fury Gap, their last carbide lamp went out and the worst of the storm struck with a force that almost pinned them to the rocks.

Munday graphically described it this way: "Rain, hail and snow lashed us mercilessly. Rocks and ice roaring down from the lightning-smitten crags swelled the echoing crashes of thunder. Jutting rocks spurted livid flame for minutes at a time. Our wet clothing sent off ghostly flashes. Our ice-axes hissed and sputtered with fans of flames up to three inches long, and my hat was fringed with pendant, dancing fire. These fireworks continued for three hours.

"We tried to shelter under an overhanging rock, but the only footing was boulders wedged uncertainly in a great crack below, so we soon forsook its doubtful security. Going down by dropping recklessly from rock to rock, half blinded by alternate brilliance and blackness, somehow we escaped anything worse than bruises and torn clothes." Yet another storm then pinned them to camp for a week, and their attempts for that year were finished.

On July 8, 1928, the most persistent husband-and-wife climbing team in Canadian history was back with Don Munday's brother Bert. Once more they began the long climb up the jagged West Ridge. Once more it was late in the day when they got to the bottom of the final 400-foot slope. But this time the weather was good, and they were able to finish the job. At 7.45 p.m. they stood on the top of the north-west peak of Mount Waddington, almost exactly 13,000 feet high.

It was a most impressive and inspiring place to be, commanding by its eminence a view of more than 20,000 square miles of some of the toughest and wildest country in the world. But it was not the view at their feet that fascinated them. This, wrote Munday, "held our gaze less than the ice-encrusted rock spire of Waddington, its last 600 feet grimly impregnable. It must be seen at close range to be believed — then it is hard to believe.

"The white fang (on which we stood) tapered suddenly to a fragile tip on which one person might stand. Beyond it a few hundred yards away across the void, and perhaps 60 feet higher, poised the highest peak of Waddington, almost a nightmare in its grim inaccessibility, in its terrific upthrust, in its baffling rock structure peculiar to the central mass of the mountain.

"And for further mockery of the mountaineer, the mountain ceaselessly combs moisture from the winds to drape the upper rocks, too sheer for snow to cling, with plates and plumes and festoons of huge crumbling ice feathers. Our present peak was merely such a plume, with blue light coming up between our feet."

The gap between, the one through which Hillary and I flew in 1955, seemed unclimbable, Munday decided, and was out of the question under that year's conditions as a way of getting onto the final main tower.

In the next few years the Mundays returned regularly to the Waddington area, exploring, mapping, and climbing many of the peaks. Munday wrote prolifically about their adventures, and climbers throughout North America began to take particular notice. Gradually other mountaineers began to visit this wild and fascinating apex of the Coast Range. Various parties prospected different approaches, and Waddington was becoming one of the best-known unclimbed mountains on the continent.

Then, in 1934, widespread attention was focused on the peak when a first-class climber was killed there while attempting a route near the one on which Mrs. Munday and her sister had been so battered by falling rocks in 1927.

Alec Dalgleish, a twenty-six-year-old Vancouver telephone engineer and promising artist, was one of a very strong party of four climbers that was just beginning its first assault on the peak. His companions were Alan Lambert, Dr. Neal M. Carter, and Eric Brooks, all of whom became distinguished Canadian mountaineers.

Early on June 26, they climbed a steep 600-foot snow gully leading to a buttress of rock that joined the south-east ridge about half-way between Waddington and the pass between it and Spearmen Peak. Two ropes were tied together, and as they reached the broken rocks of the buttress Lambert first took the lead.

All were roughly equal in skill; so when Lambert had used up all his rope and reached a safe spot, Dalgleish, who was at the other end of the rope, climbed up to him and kept on going until he was in the lead. Resting-points became scarcer as they went up. Dr. Carter untied from the rope and stepped aside, giving Dalgleish more slack to move up and examine a spot just above, where the promising route seemed almost to evaporate. This left Brooks belaying Dalgleish, solidly anchored on a ledge, and paying out the rope over his shoulder as he kept a watchful eye on the leader fifty feet above him.

Lambert then untied from his inactive end of the rope and went up to Dalgleish, and they both took a thorough look at the prospect ahead. They decided they would be able to go no higher in safety, and should turn around. They were at about 10,500 feet, it was barely noon, and they had lots of time to try another route that started at a fork in the gully a few feet lower.

Lambert descended unroped, safely and with apparent ease, to a small ledge just above Carter and Brooks. Then Dalgleish began to come down, using the same route. Carter and Brooks took in the rope that became slack as he descended, carefully keeping it out of the way of his feet.

He was within thirty feet of them when Lambert heard a slight scratching of nailed boots on the rock and looked quickly up. He was horrified to see Dalgleish disappearing over the angle of rock between the buttress face and the cliff that formed one wall of the snow gully. Not a sound came from Dalgleish as he fell. Brooks pulled furiously at the rope, trying to gather in the slack before Dalgleish went very far. But he had pulled only a few feet when there was a tremendous jerk on the rope that almost whipped him off his feet. The rope slid down the sharp edge of a shattered rock, and severed only a few feet from their unbelieving eyes.

Seconds later they saw him rolling and bouncing down the steep gully almost beneath their feet. It took the three men more than three hours to reach him, and they found that he had died instantly when he slammed into the cliff wall. Analysing the accident later, after Dalgleish had been buried near by and a cairn erected to his memory, Dr. Carter suggested that the rope itself, the most important safeguard of the mountaineer, might have caused the death. Dalgleish fell free of the cliffs for about sixty feet until the tightening rope slammed him into the rock wall, he said. Then he fell free into the soft snow of the gully a hundred feet below. "A straight fall into the snow would have been serious," Dr. Carter summed up, "but not extremely so. If stunned, the descent down the gully would not have ended disastrously, judging from the course actually taken."

The day after the accident, and knowing nothing of it, another party reached within 800 feet of the summit, climbing from the unknown north side. This party consisted of Ferris and Roger Neave and Campbell Secord, from Winnipeg. Bad weather plagued them as they tried to scratch their way up ice-coated rocks. When they were finally defeated, they hammered iron pegs called pitons into cracks in the rock. Each piton had a ring in the end, through which they threaded the rope until it was doubled. Then they lowered themselves down one at a time, in the spectacular-looking but very safe method called rappelling. The rate of descent is controlled by the friction the rope develops from being wrapped around the body, and by a light grip of one hand. When the last man was down the first section, he pulled one end of the rope until it came free of the piton. Another piton was hammered home, and the process began again.

It was dark when they got off the rocks onto the snow, and they spent the night above 12,000 feet huddled together in an ice-cave just inside the bergschrund, the giant crevasse formed where the ice pulls away from the cliffs of the summit tower.

In July, the Mundays were back again, this time with Henry Hall, who had climbed on Logan three years earlier, professional guide Hans Fuhrer, Philip Brock, and Ronald Munro. Their climbs on near-by peaks had given the Mundays unrivalled knowledge of Waddington in all its ever-changing moods and aspects. Now they felt that the northeast face, where the Neave party had climbed a short while before, offered the best chance of success. But each time they had seen this precipice, ever-sheltered from the sun, it had been thickly coated with ice. They decided first to climb again up the north-west peak, to examine their prospective route closely. They reached the lower peak on August 13, and found the summit steeple in good condition – by

Waddington standards, anyway. But still ice-feathers several feet thick draped the vertical rocks of the upper section, plastered on layer by layer in storms, with seldom a thaw to pry them free.

This time they were able to find a route that would take them from the north-west peak on a line beneath the celebrated gap and then onto the rocks of the tower 600 feet or so beneath the tip. The last 600 feet, however, were judged so severe and exposed that they thought it was unjustifiable to attempt it without a large number of pitons which they could hammer in for safeguards at almost every step. As each piton is pounded in, the leader is able to tie himself to it, so that even when he hasn't an adequate ledge to stand on he can still bring up the next man in safety. He is anchored firmly against a fall.

Four of the party were among the most experienced mountaineers in North America. They carefully discussed all the aspects of the terrifying summit; then, for the conservative *Canadian Alpine Journal,* Don Munday wrote: "For the present, Mt. Waddington deserves to be rated as verging on the impossible when all factors are taken into account."

In *The Times* of London, Munday wrote: "Hans now shared our belief that it defied ordinary climbing methods. He solemnly agreed that the mountain would not spare the over-daring and commended our decision not to attempt Mt. Waddington again.

"Eight seasons of effort under the shadow of Mt. Waddington, Mystery Mountain still, were closed for my wife and me. Some disappointment there must be, but also a deep, strange elation that the mountain had proved so great."

When Hall spoke to reporters in Vancouver later, he was far from conservative about it. "When we report this to the American Alpine Club, I only hope it does not fire a number of foolish attempts," he said. "I don't want to see anyone try that tower peak of Waddington because I think someone will get killed. I think it is impossible." Hans Fuhrer, a professional with an outstanding record, nodded his head emphatically in agreement.

Around this time, too, the death of Dalgleish had revived stories that Waddington was a "hoodoo" peak. Certainly there were quite a few incidents to give strength to this. Within eight months of the first expedition, Johnson and Agur, two of its members, were caught in a big avalanche in the mountains overlooking Vancouver. Agur was killed.

51

The head packer of Henry Hall's party in 1933 was murdered shortly after he came out of the area. A. E. Roovers, a member of the same party, was killed in a climbing accident elsewhere. Mrs. Munday was badly battered, and Dr. Carter was injured by an accident on the boat taking him home after the death of Dalgleish.

All this, however, did nothing to discourage attempts on the mountain. In fact, it spurred them on. The peak became the most sought-after climbing prize on the continent, and the Vancouver newspapers printed story after story of expeditions planning to climb the peak that Munday had called "a nightmare moulded in rock".

Hall's warning in the 1934 *American Alpine Journal* specifically brought the Sierra Club of California into the picture. Richard M. Leonard, chairman of the club's committee on rock-climbing, wrote that the article "brought a realization that in the Coast Mountains of B.C. existed a peak that from the defences it had been able to offer must now take rank as one of the major peaks of America." Here, he decided, was a chance for his rock-climbing experts, to whom the impossible took just a little longer, to try "new methods, both in technique and equipment".

Eight Sierra men, led by Bestor Robinson, and including Leonard, made their first attack in 1935. They found that the "impossible" assessment of Waddington was true for them, at least that year. They made three attempts on the main summit without even reaching the main problems. Then they climbed the north-west peak and set up camp only 700 feet beneath it, with the idea of crossing to the main tower below the gap. Don Woods, a member of the party, wrote: "The view from the summit was both stupendous and appalling. The rock tower, only 60 feet higher than our snow summit, loomed up a thousand feet away, and looked extremely difficult with its fresh ice and snow." Within hours a savage storm routed them from their eyrie on the peak, and they fled down to safety, their attempt finished.

Dick Leonard summed it up ruefully: "We had felt that rock climbing would be of great importance in the solution of the problem. We are still of that opinion. As a pure rock climb, shorn of its defences of ice, snow, avalanches and storm, Mt. Waddington would still be a formidable opponent. However, we feel that given reasonable weather it can be climbed. We have made much longer and far more difficult rock climbs in the Yosemite Valley.

"It is the snow and ice on every ledge, the falling ice from far above, and the sudden storms that make Mt. Waddington a problem that may only be solved in some season of extraordinarily long periods of clear weather. If an expert party of rock climbers with full piton equipment could ever find a day when the southwest face was free of ice, they could climb rapidly up to the final summit pitch.

"There, at an altitude of over 13,000 feet, it is safe to assume they would still find Waddington's final defence, the ice-feathers, coating each pinnacle and every face of the summit arête, even the overhangs. The highest degree of care and skill would be required to devise a type of technique which would be effective and safe. Whether the ice-feathers can be passed, we cannot say. One can only know when one gets that far."

Leonard was anxious to get that far, and he came back in 1936. It had been arranged that the Sierra Club and the B.C. Mountaineering Club would put a joint party of picked climbers on the peak for an all-out attempt in 1936. Six were chosen: Robinson, Leonard, and Jack Riegelhuth, representing the Sierra Club; and Bill Dobson, Jim Irving, and Lawrence Grassi, representing Canadian climbers. All the plans were made on this basis, but when Robinson arrived, he brought three more climbers – Hervey Voge, Kenneth Adam, and Raffi Bedayan.

The two groups, never a team, went their separate ways at the summit tower on July 19. The Canadians took the westerly side of the face, just to the right of a gully that runs up to the gap between the twin summits. Leading their rope of three was Grassi, a stocky miner, of Italian descent, from Canmore, Alberta. He was forty-six, and his reputation as a rock-climber was outstanding. He made many difficult and dangerous climbs alone, and for him the freedom of the hills was a complete contrast with his early work in dark and restricted coal mines. Hours passed as they moved slowly but safely up the ever-steepening rock. When they stopped for lunch, they were still 1,700 feet below the summit, and the worst was yet to come. At this point, Irving's knee, which had caused him trouble all the way from the inlet, became so bad that he would no longer trust it.

He offered to rope into the big gully and make his way down alone. Grassi, the expert at lone climbing, who knew its problems better than most, emphatically refused to permit this. "On this mountain," he said, "we go up and down together."

53

Irving insisted, but Grassi would go no further than a slight compromise. He finally conceded that Irving could stay in safety where he was, while the other two would prospect a little higher. They climbed another 400 feet; then all three returned to camp.

The Sierra Club men also failed. They took the south-east side of the tower, and reached an estimated 12,500 feet before they were blocked by an unclimbable section. Almost 800 feet of the toughest climbing still lay beyond — with the final ice-feather ramparts that Leonard feared still waiting for those who could overcome the rock-climbing problems.

For each party, this was to have been merely the first attempt of the season. As it turned out, two polite men waiting on the glacier below made it their last chance to make the first ascent. The two men were Fritz Wiessner and William House, two of the finest climbers the United States has ever produced. Wiessner, a thirty-six-year-old chemist from New York, had been a member of the 1932 German-American expedition to Nanga Parbat, the killer peak of 26,660 feet in the Himalayas. As that expedition was finishing, a tower of ice collapsed, hurling him sixty feet into a crevasse. Although he was in shock, badly bruised, and could use only one arm, he detached himself from the rope and cut steps up an overhanging ice-wall to safety.

He had climbed in many of the world's great ranges, and made first ascents of impossible-looking rock spires in Wyoming. Three years later, he was to be leader of the American expedition to K2, the second highest mountain in the world, and was to reach 27,500 feet, a mere 750 feet from the summit. A stocky, powerful man, he was absolutely fearless. In fact, one critic suggested after the K2 attempt that the expedition was badly unbalanced because Wiessner was so much stronger and better than anybody else on it.

Wiessner's companion on Waddington was William House, a slim, graceful rock-climber who made the almost impossible seem commonplace as he moved delicately up precipices. He, too, was destined for K2. He reached 25,000 feet in 1938, and at 21,500 feet did the most important "lead" of the expedition. When the route was in danger of petering out at the base of a steep cliff, he forced a route up a steep, difficult chimney that was ever afterwards known to climbers as House's Chimney.

House and Wiessner, with Alanson Willcox and Elizabeth Woolsey, who was a fine climber and an American Olympic skier, had actually been on the ground before the other parties. But, as some of the other party's climbers had been on Waddington before, Wiessner's group generously conformed with the climbing custom that they should be allowed to make the first attempt at it this season.

Wiessner and House, who were to make the first attempt for their group, moved their small tent up onto Dais Glacier, just 400 feet from the foot of the rock tower. As the British Columbia climbers came by, they thanked the Americans for their courtesy, and told them it was now their turn. The Sierra men did the same when they stumbled by the tent at midnight. So at 3.30 a.m. on July 20, the pair set off. Quickly and safely they climbed up the big gully leading to the gap. Then, when they were less than 300 feet below the gap, they tried to climb the 150-foot vertical wall of the gully, which would land them on the sweeping cliffs of the south face. But the wall was of rotten rock, with every ledge and bump on it covered in slick, clear ice. They were fearless, but not fools, and they retreated, disappointed.

Next day they tried again, while the other parties still rested below, watching their incredible progress. It was, said one of the watchers, a wild route they took to the summit that flared like a flame above one of the loneliest places on earth.

This time, Wiessner and House went farther right, to another gully that rose steeply to a gap just east of the main summit — between it and a jagged tooth that was almost as high. The snow in the gully was steep — almost sixty degrees — yet they moved together in perfect rhythm, finding that their crampons bit perfectly into the hard snow. They climbed out of the gully, and then edged slowly left across rotten rock to cover almost the entire width of the south face. By 7 a.m. they were at the upper end of a small triangular snow patch, close to where they would have reached the face had they been able to climb out of the earlier gully.

In the centre of the snow patch was a warning of the dangers they had to face steadily on this terrible tower. A deep channel ran down the centre of it, gouged by a constant fall of rocks and brittle icicles.

They crossed it one at a time, each belayed by the other, who paid out the rope around the ice-axe, which was firmly buried in the snow as an anchor. Each was ready to leap out of the channel and swing on the dizzy rope if another fall began as he crossed. They were well satisfied with the progress they had made so far, even though they realized that the real problems were yet to come.

Wiessner later recorded his feelings at this point: "Above us extended the last 1,000 feet of the south face in sheer, forbidding-looking rocks, but the possibility of climbing it could be detected by anyone looking at it with a trained eye . . . .

"Mentally and physically I was keyed up to the very high pitch which one reaches on certain occasions; at this time I knew that the summit would be ours. Determined, and feeling that today no obstacle of a technical nature could stop us, I started on the rocks."

The climbing was severe as soon as he started, and very soon he had to change from his nailed climbing-boots to rope-soled boots. These hold better on almost-non-existent friction holds, when only the friction of the soles on smooth rock, and the balance, can support the climber. The small ledges they had been able to use up to the snow patch were now getting rapidly less inviting. They were too small to rest on, and barely big enough to balance on – and the drop below loomed ever greater. Wiessner passed back his boots, extra rope, and ice-axe to House so that he would be better able to keep in balance. There was no rope above him, in case of a fall. Every rope's length now Wiessner had to drive in a piton to which he could tie himself for safety while he brought House up.

Hours slipped by unheeded as they worked out the right combination of small and loose holds that would keep them from hurtling 1,500 feet to the glacier. In places, the shattered rock was so loose that the very brush of the light rope against it was enough to tumble pieces end over end through the cold, clear air. One overhanging wall demanded all the nerve and skill of a professional high-wire acrobat. As Wiessner went at it, with the continuity, almost fluidity, of movement that alone makes such things possible, he found that the tiny cracks that served as holds were covered with ice. But on this day nothing could stop him. On he went.

Now they were on the last 500-foot wall leading to the summit. Here, said Wiessner, "for three rope-lengths the climbing reached the upper limit of the technically possible". Several hours went by as he struggled with this crux of the climb – hours which House spent tied to a piton directly below the leader, a helpless target for any rocks that Wiessner might dislodge. If Wiessner slipped now, the lives of both, linked by the rope, depended entirely on the slim iron piton hammered home into the rock. House was tied to it, Wiessner tied to him.

Right above their heads now their route joined the summit ridge, only one hundred easy feet from the tip. Twenty feet short of the junction, the mountain put the last obstacle in their way — another overhanging bulge of rock that could not be avoided. Wiessner was climbing now like a man inspired, a precision machine to which problems meant only solutions. He was over it with hardly a ripple in his flow of movement, and minutes later the two men were only twenty feet from the summit.

It was a classic summit — barely big enough for one man to stand on. They stood on it one at a time, each safeguarding the other from a stance twenty feet below. The time was 3.40 p.m., thirteen hours from the time they had left the camp.

Of his feelings at this moment of triumph, Wiessner wrote tersely: "We were rewarded with a grand view of the beautiful Coast Mountains which extended around us." In mountaineering, as in so many other endeavours of life, it is better to travel hopefully than to arrive.

Quickly they built a small stone cairn where they stood, which was the only place to put one, and then began thinking of how to get down. Their original plan had been to rope down from the peak over the north face, lowering themselves from one piton to another with the 125-foot climbing-rope and the 300-foot spare rope they had brought. But one look at its ice-encrusted rocks discouraged them, and they decided to retrace the airy route up which they had climbed.

The ropes were quickly laid out and down they went, House first. As they lowered themselves, they found that in many places the rope hung free of the rocks, dangling in space, striking evidence of the calibre and angle of their climb. Finding a safe spot to start each rappel took time, and it was almost dark when they regained the triangular snow patch 1,000 feet down. They felt their way off the rest of the cliffs in the darkness, occasionally cringing as fusillades of ice and rock fell near them from above. It was past 2 a.m. when they got back to camp, after twenty-three hours of severe and sensational climbing.

History had been made that was to cause a variety of emotions in the mountaineering world. But it was to be some time before the outside climbers were to hear of it. Wiessner had made no arrangement for rushing off to civilization with the news, even though Miss Woolsey was a well-known newspaper reporter. They preferred to carry on climbing and leave the writing until later.

The well-organized British Columbia expedition had its own reporter with it, Arthur Mayse of the *Vancouver Daily Province*. He had brought a crate of homing pigeons with him, packing it complainingly through the bush and the snow-storms. Now he scribbled the news on thin rice-paper, fixed a copy to a leg of each bird, and set them all free. Up they soared, in high, ecstatic circles, and headed for home, 175 miles away. That was the last that anybody ever saw of them. The Coast Range's giant eagles apparently killed them all.

When Wiessner finally wrote of his ascent of the steeple-like summit, he said: "In twenty years of climbing I have never encountered a harder mountain for its altitude. That goes for the Alps, in Europe, or anywhere else. To my knowledge, none of the big mountains over 13,000 feet that have been climbed anywhere is as difficult to climb by its easiest route as Waddington is [by its easiest route]."

Their route has never been duplicated. In 1942, two brilliant climbing brothers from Seattle, Fred and Helmy Beckey, made the only other ascent of the south face. In parts they followed the Wiessner route, in others they made safer variations. It was 8.30 at night when they reached the top, and they spent the night on a ledge 150 feet below the summit, tied to pitons so they would not roll off when they dozed. All next day they climbed down. Then, when they were 400 feet above the base of the rocks, a falling rock hit Helmy above the knee. His muscle was damaged and a severed vein bled profusely. They spent yet another night out before they staggered down to safety.

Helmy Beckey was seventeen the day the rock hit his knee. He wrote of his experience: "The ice and rockfall danger is so great on the south face that I believe it is hardly a justifiable climb. Future parties might find both shorter and safer climbing on the north or east faces."

Future parties did – but in the next fifteen years, despite many attempts, only two parties, comprising six men, were successful. Hillary himself spotted a route on the north side, and said that the next time he came through Vancouver, he would take time out and try to climb it. But he said, "I hope you Canadians do it first, though."

In 1958, when British Columbia was celebrating its centenary, a Canadian party finally climbed the main tower of Waddington. Five men, led by Adolph Bitterlich of the Alpine Club of Canada, making his third attempt, climbed it by the north face and the north-east ridge. With Bitterlich were his brother Ulf, John Owen, Arno Meier, and Christian Schiel, all but Owen comparative newcomers to British Columbia.

During the years since then, the tempo of climbing on Mount Waddington has stepped up considerably. Almost every year brings new plane-loads of mountaineers from Canada and the United States eager to assault the scores of fine peaks that make "Mundayland" an enchanting lure for the climber. The toll, however, has been high.

In 1960, John Owen, a tireless young man of twenty-four with the ambition to earn a guide's diploma in Europe, returned to the peak. With him were Derrick Boddy, a talented English rock-climber, Elfrida Pigou, and Joan Stirling, who hoped to be the first women up the main tower. At 8,200 feet, a toppling ice-wall buried all four, and their bodies were never found. A few weeks later, knowing nothing of the tragedy, the first woman, Virginia Gill Mohling, did climb the main tower.

In 1962, when I first went to Waddington, no fewer than nine climbers reached the top of the tower – one more than in the whole twenty years after the first ascent. For the first time, a whole rope of Canadian-born climbers made it: Ken Baker, with a guide's certificate in the Rockies, Byron Olson, and Dr. David Kennedy. And tiny, Swiss-born Mrs. Esther Kafer, mother of two, became the first Canadian woman on the summit. It was a family affair. Leading a second rope right behind her was her husband, Martin.

Times have changed, but not the mountain. As I sat with Mrs. Kafer and the others on the Munday's north-west peak, which we had gained by a route not climbed before, the tower looming 1,000 feet away still looked as fierce as when Munday saw it in 1928.

He said then, "It must be seen at close range to be believed – then it is hard to believe."

An Air Liner Vanishes

MOUNT SLESSE

The magnificent Coast Range and Cascade Mountains of British Columbia are a delight and a challenge to the mountaineer. To the airman, they are a menace. In perfect weather, the myriad snow-capped peaks, the rich, variant greens of the valleys, and the meandering threads of rivers far below make for the airborne passenger an enthralling glimpse of a world apart.

But the weather is seldom perfect, or even good for more than a few scant hours at a time. Mountains brew their own fantastic storms, and in hours the change can be as drastic as that from heaven into hell.

Throughout the fall and winter a succession of Pacific storms push great oceans of wet, mild air over the shoreline. It rains as each mass comes in. Vancouver Airport, ten miles from where the North Shore mountains rear from the water, averages forty inches of rain a year. The city hall, half-way between, has fifty-one inches. And the North Shore, damp dormitory of the city worker, has over eighty. Yet even this is comparatively moderate. Up-coast at well-named Ocean Falls, the average is more than 170 inches.

The mountains force the incoming ocean of air to rise. As this air rises, it cools and can hold less moisture; so it rains some more — or snows. So far, apart from causing occasional floods and constant grumbling, the heavy rain is beneficial. It feeds the giant trees that provide British Columbia's staple industry. The snow becomes an alpine reservoir, releasing its liquid gold in the summer to provide a wealth of hydro-electric potential.

But the phenomenon that generates probably the most energy is worthless to man or beast — and dangerous. As the storms sweep in from the ocean, they batter on the precipice walls of the mountains and are hurled abruptly upwards. The air becomes violently turbulent as it screams over the mountain ridges. It is, rather paradoxically, even more turbulent on the lee or sheltered side of the mountain. The ridges act in the same way as rocks in a fast-moving torrent of water. Pressure builds up on the up-stream side, and the water hurls itself over the top faster than ever. On the down-stream side the flow disintegrates into a whirling, down-circling maelstrom. So it is with the torrent of air on the mountains. Fierce wind currents may race from any angle. The spinning air masses may cause subsidence which lets an aircraft, even the biggest, drop with a sickening jolt, rather as if the floor had collapsed beneath it.

Combined with this, the sudden chilling of very damp air as it rises may lead to icing — which can plaster an aircraft in a very few minutes with a solid layer of ice. This adds very considerably to the weight, and by disrupting the designed air-flow decreases the wing's ability to lift the plane.

To avoid all this, light aircraft seek out low mountain passes when the weather is doubtful, and often try to fly below the weather by following twisting valleys. The Fraser Valley is a favourite route in southern British Columbia. At the head of the lower valley, ninety-nine road miles from Vancouver, is the little village of Hope, in a strikingly beautiful setting. From there, a spectacular mountain highway climbs east to Princeton, eighty-three miles away, crossing two passes of almost 4,500 feet on the way. Here the abrupt mountains suddenly die and the rolling uplands of the Interior plateau stretch for many miles.

The 120 air miles from Vancouver to Princeton have lured very many fliers to their deaths. Many of their planes have never been found, and the area is widely known by its grim reputation as "The

Graveyard of the Air". Dozens of pilots have been trapped there by the weather and their own temerity. It all happens so easily. A pilot runs into solid cloud ahead, and quickly turns to head for home – only to find that in minutes the evil magic of condensation has packed with clouds the valley behind him too. The noose takes little time to tighten. Or he flies through a hole in the clouds to get over a shrouded high spot – and then the layer of clouds turns solid. He cannot find a way back down.

Finally, cautiously, guessing where he is, he begins to let down through the layer. Airmen have a brutal piece of jargon that masks in a joke the splintering agony of hitting a cloud-wreathed mountainside. The erring pilot, they say, just flies into a "cumulo-granitus" cloud.

Light aeroplanes generally stay far away from cloud. In fact entering cloud is specifically banned unless the pilot is trained and checked out in blind flying by instruments alone, a highly specialized art.

The commercial air liners cannot afford to stop for every storm. All their pilots are instrument experts, and they push on in safety when they can barely see their own wing-tips. The air liners have the extra power to carry big loads of ice, yet climb far above the clouds and mountains. Without even looking at their maps, the pilots can follow "radio ranges". These are the invisible highways of the sky that guide them through darkness and storms. Right across the mountains – and the rest of the country too – is a chain of radio stations.

Each one, about one hundred miles from its nearest neighbour, sends out a narrow line of signals. When the pilot is right in the centre of the line, he hears a steady humming sound on his radio. Up to five miles to one side of the centre, he hears also a steady dit-da, the Morse code signal for the letter "A". Up to five miles on the other side he hears da-dit, the Morse "N". Spaced along the route, too, are radio beacons. A needle in the cockpit automatically tells the pilot when he is over one of these or when he is passing by to one side or the other.

These are the basic guides that have led our commercial air liners through the night, though radar and newer radio aids are gradually replacing them. But despite these aids, the "Graveyard of the Air" has continued to take its toll. It probably always will.

The most savage-looking spire in this region is Mount Slesse, a steeple of rock 8,200 feet high that has always been a considerable challenge to mountaineers. In the summer of 1956, Elfrida Pigou reached the top of it. But on that day the climb was through cloud and the difficult summit had no value as a viewpoint. On that day, too, she had followed someone else up the steep rock pitches. To the purist, being anywhere else but first on the rope sometimes tends to detract from the satisfaction of difficult climbing. So she decided to climb it again, in clear weather so that she could enjoy the beauty of the warm spring sun on the rock and the diamond glitter of its light on the snow – and at the head of her own rope, which would finally give her the feeling that she really had climbed Slesse.

Note that the word is "climbed", not "conquered". There are people who feel they "conquer" difficult peaks and thereby prove their superiority over lesser men and nature. Elfrida Pigou was not one of them. Her love of nature's sterner aspects was deep, and her knowledge of them such that she knew "conquest" of mountains can come only when a beneficent nature lowers her guard. There is, of course, a conquest involved in climbing all difficult mountains: the conquest of one's own weaknesses, and the steady stretching of man's petty limits.

It was not hard to find companions for her trip in the spring of 1957. The spire of Slesse is a constant challenge to climbers, but few knew enough about the area to lead a trip. When a leader comes looking for volunteers, there is usually no shortage. So it was this time. On Saturday, May 11, she left Vancouver with Geoffrey Walker, 28, an English draftsman, and David Cathcart, 23, an Irish civil engineer. Walker had been in the country several years, but it was only the third Canadian climbing trip for Cathcart. In fact he had arrived in Vancouver only six weeks before, from his native Ballymena, Northern Ireland.

One of the first things he had done was to join the Vancouver Section of the Alpine Club of Canada. He was delighted now that Miss Pigou asked him to go along. He did not know many members of the club yet, but he already knew of her reputation as a very determined and quite indefatigable climber.

She looked diminutive and almost frail. But she had been on expeditions that had made the first ascents of 10,000-foot peaks in the jungle-guarded tangle of the Coast Range. It was more or less a Club joke that if you saw a giant-sized packsack making its way through the thickest bush, apparently unsupported, it was no mirage. Somewhere underneath were the ninety-five pounds of nerve and whipcord that

63

made up Elfrida Pigou. I have seen her carry packs so heavy she could not lift them off the ground. But provided somebody else would raise them up high enough for her to slip into the shoulder straps, she would carry them for hours.

The route the party took to Slesse was the usual approach, up the Fraser Valley to Chilliwack, then south on the road to Cultus Lake. At Vedder Crossing a logging road swings east along the south side of the Chilliwack River, famous for its steelhead fishing. It is a rough road. But in recent years, prison inmates have established forest camps there, and as a rehabilitation project have been rebuilding the road towards Chilliwack Lake, which is set in a beautiful cirque of mountains.

The three climbers had not gone very far before they came to a sign reading "Road Closed". Fortunately there was a workman near by to tell them they could get through safely, and they pushed slowly on.

The base camp was up Slesse Creek, five miles from where they had to leave the car. It consisted of a couple of decrepit, long-abandoned shacks at the 1,900-foot level, where they settled down for the night.

At 6 a.m. on Sunday, May 12, they set out to tackle the jagged pinnacles of Slesse, which still towered 6,300 feet above them. This is a long way to climb in a day, particularly if the going is hard. In the Alps or the Canadian Rockies, with their higher inland valleys, a peak with such a vertical uplift would be of the order of 10,000 to 11,000 feet high.

The going was rough from the start, from the moment they balanced precariously across two rotten logs spanning tumultuous Slesse Creek. The western slope of the mountain was tricky, with wet, slippery snow masking logs and boulders – the sort of place where it is quick and simple to break a leg by a misplaced step. Fortunately, as they went higher, the snow became firmer, and held the climbing boot more safely. At 4,500 feet, the going began to get reasonable. But to counteract this advantage, they had now reached the bottom of the clouds. It was cold and gloomy, but often, in the mountains, a rising wind will whisk away the clouds and open up the sky in minutes. Or, even better, the climber often goes right through a layer of cloud. Then the dark world below is blotted out. Life takes on a new dimension as the fiddling problems of our artificial world are smothered for a while in the unseen cities below. The fundamental mountains take on an ever greater, glittering majesty as the sun reflects from the top of the clouds and helps light the dark canyons that brood around the austere slopes.

So, despite the cloud, they pushed on, plodding slowly through the steep snow. The whole west side of the mountain is seamed, like a wrinkled face, with gullies, all looking much alike in the fog. Elfrida chose a likely-looking one and up they went.

Fate, or chance, or sheer blind luck, had set the stage. And within minutes the drama opened. As they climbed steadily, Walker spotted a piece of paper on the snow. He picked it up and found it was a Trans-Canada Air Lines map of radio beams and approaches to the airfield at Sydney, Nova Scotia, at the other side of Canada.

"We didn't think much of it at the time," he said later. "It seemed quite dry and perfectly clean. It could have been dropped quite recently."

There was nothing else around, so they continued up. Cathcart was not feeling too well, and when they reached a notch in the summit ridge he settled down in a safe spot to rest and wait for the others. It was about 7,300 feet, and the spot was a flattish, snow-covered saddle between two very impressive walls of rock. The time: about 1.15 p.m.

By now Elfrida had realized she was in the wrong gully, to the south of the one she had used on her previous climb. But it was too late to turn back — and there was always the chance of finding a new route to the summit. The going was harder now as the pair turned north and headed towards the next pinnacle.

Right from the saddle rose a steep rock wall, which they quickly climbed. In the centre was a short pitch with an awkward move in the middle of a vertical wall. But soon they were over it and the slope leaned back considerably.

Then Elfrida spotted something lying in the snow a few feet ahead. It was a twisted, fractured piece of aluminum about eighteen inches long, with rivets and a few small fittings attached. It lay about ten feet below the actual crest of the ridge. Excitedly they began to hunt among the clouds, but found nothing as big as the first piece. There were tiny bits of plywood, a blue and yellow piece of metal, a few feet of sewing-thread wrapped around a piece of paper.

They put it all into a small pile, built a little cairn of rocks to mark the place, and then pushed on. Only a few feet higher they reached the finger-like top of a subsidiary peak about 7,700 feet high, south of the main mass of Slesse's summit. To the north, their pinnacle dropped off sheer. To the east were the impossible cliffs, with cloud masking all but the nearest few feet. They decided to turn back. In that weather there was no other sensible choice.

At the saddle, Cathcart was feeling cold, still sick, and a little worried. The others had been away now for two and three-quarter hours. He had not expected them to be nearly so long. He had no way of knowing what had happened to them. If anything had, he would have a miserable, nerve-wracking time making his way out alone.

Then suddenly they appeared, "yelling and waving the bit of metal. I wasn't surprised at all. After Geoffrey discovered the landing instructions, I felt sure there was a wreck on one of the nearby peaks."

There was a mild argument now about what to do with the metal. It carried a series of numbers and the letters "TCA", and the men wanted to make a note of these and take the information down to the authorities. Elfrida insisted that the authorities should see the numbers and the piece of wreckage for themselves. It was jagged and sharp, and cumbersome to carry through the bush, but as the boys joked about her enthusiasm, she tied it onto her pack and they set off down.

The descent was cold and unpleasant, and heavy rain had soaked them by the time they reached the cabins about 8 p.m. They quickly ate, walked out to the car, and drove home. It was after 2 a.m. when Elfrida reached there, and, she felt, much too late to wake anybody up to tell them about a piece of metal.

As soon as she got up the next morning, she telephoned me. She called me first because I was one of the three Alpine Club members on the executive of the Mountain Rescue Group. One Vancouver newspaper made mysterious noises about the "long delay" in reporting the discovery. The suggestion was, I suppose, that as a newspaperman I had kept it all a secret so that I could have an exclusive story.

Minutes after Miss Pigou finally reached me at the office, on her third or fourth try, I was on the way to collect the piece of aluminum from her. As soon as I saw what it was, I stopped at my home near by and collected my mountaineering equipment. When I got back to the office, I telephoned Norman Donnelly, operations chief of Trans-Canada Air Lines (now Air Canada), who asked me to take the fragment to his office right away.

At the airport, his office was jammed with officials of the various agencies connected with air search-and-rescue operations. Already they had confirmed the numbers from the bit of wreckage, and identified it as part of the under-side of a wing.

At long last, and quite by chance, the first clue had been found to Canada's most terrible and mystifying air disaster up to that time. On the night of Sunday, December 9, 1956, a four-engined North Star air liner simply vanished. Aboard were fifty-nine passengers and a crew of three. For five months the peaks and their shroud of snow completely buried the secret of one of the worst air disasters in the world.

The tragic flight had begun, of course, as just another routine trip. Captain Allen Jack Clark did not need to be formally told that the weather was bad that Sunday. It had been raining much harder than usual, even for Vancouver in December, which is saying a lot. The strong winds at ground level told him that a very active storm was working above. He met his first officer, Terry Boon, at the airport, and together they strolled at 4.45 p.m. into the aviation weather-forecaster's office. Meteorologist Don McMullen was busy at the cross-section drawing he had made of the three-dimensional weather, so important to pilots.

Allen Clark looked at it and grinned. "The black pencil isn't bad enough today," he said; "you have to use red ones." The red lines on the drawing showed the places where he was likely to run into icing conditions.

On the west side of the Cascades, the side through which he had to fly first to get to Calgary and the east, the cloud started at 1,500 feet, and continued right up to 19,000 feet. Another TCA flight that had come in a little earlier from the same route reported icing in the clouds at 14,000 feet. So it was suggested that Clark should take his Flight 810 to about 19,000 feet for his trip. At this level, said McMullen, Clark would have a tail wind of almost 100 m.p.h. His first stop was to be Calgary, in the foothills of the Rocky Mountains, but the forecast there was not too good either. However, Regina, Saskatoon, and Winnipeg were clear and would stay open if he decided he could not stop at Calgary.

Bad as it seemed to the layman, such weather was old stuff to 35-year-old Allen Clark and his co-pilot. Clark had been a bomber captain during the war, and joined TCA in January 1945. His long experience and spells as an RCAF instructor brought him rapid promotion, and he was made a captain on June 7, 1946. He had been flying this route since June 1955 and knew it thoroughly. In North Stars alone he had flown nearly 1,000,000 miles – and they accounted for only one-quarter of his total flying time.

His flying life was ruled by a pilot's axiom that is fundamental: "There are old pilots and there are bold pilots. But there are no old bold pilots." It was said of Allen Clark, more or less in jest, that there had been complaints from farmers about his flying. Each day he went by, said the story, he was so exactly on course that the same few plants were in his shadow. This was stunting their growth. The story illustrates the reputation he had acquired for doing everything sensibly, just as the big book of safety rules demanded.

Terrence Boon, at twenty-six, was also a very good pilot. He too had been an instructor with the RCAF. Now he had been selected for transfer to the pride of TCA's fleet, the Viscount turbo-props. This was to be his final flight in North Stars. As he left home at the foot of the North Shore mountains, he told his mother he was looking forward to taking the rest of the year off.

Their regular stewardess was sick that day, so when Stewardess Dorothy Bjornson, 24, came in on the flight from the east, she volunteered to turn around and fly back with them. To her, unlike the others, flying was still new and exciting. The youngest of seven children, and the only girl, she had joined TCA only on July 30, after completing her training as a nurse at Winnipeg.

The plane in which they were to fly was one of the most reliable ever made. Until 1953, four-engined North Star aircraft had handled TCA's transatlantic runs. They had carried more than 4,000,000 TCA passengers since 1948, and only one plane had crashed with loss of life. This was in a mid-air collision with an RCAF training plane over Moose Jaw, Saskatchewan, in 1954, when thirty-seven people died.

Strong winds had delayed Clark's aircraft on its earlier trip from the east, and the need to make all the regulation checks helped make it about two hours later than scheduled. The crew went aboard about 5.30 p.m. to prepare for the trip. About fifteen minutes later, the passengers, some of whom were complaining mildly about the delay, began to board the big plane with the letters CF-TFD painted on its wings and tail.

Any collection of fifty-nine people selected at random presents a fascinating mixture of personalities and walks of life. This one was no exception. Best known among the passengers were five star football players. The day before, the pick of the players in Eastern Canada had met the best in the west at Vancouver in the annual Shrine all-star game.

Centre Mel Becket, 27, and Defensive End Gordon Sturtridge, 27, both members of the Saskatchewan Roughriders team, had played in the all-star game. Two of their buddies had come out to see them play – Guard Mario DeMarco, 28, and Guard Ray Syrnyk, 23. Sturtridge's wife, Mildred, was flying with him. Becket was anxious to rush home to his. She lived at Regina and was expecting their first child in a couple of weeks. All were aboard in plenty of time, but Calvin Jones, 23-year-old tackle of the Winnipeg Blue Bombers, barely made it. Jones had played with Winnipeg only one season; yet he was picked for the all-star game, and had his second-season contract in his pocket. He had slept in on Sunday morning, and missed the flight on which he was booked.

Ronald Mitchell, 23, a chemical company sales-representative, had been booked out on the flight that night at 8.30 p.m. TCA telephoned him at 2 p.m. and asked if he would prefer to go on tourist Flight 810. He agreed. Robert J. Muir, 48, well-known hardware merchant at Westview, near Powell River, was about to play Santa Claus. He was flying to Edmonton to bring his elderly mother back to the coast for Christmas. It was the sort of thing you would expect from a man whose good nature and thoughtfulness had been recognized a few months earlier by his selection as Powell River's "Good Citizen of the Year". It had been a very eventful year, too. In the September elections he had campaigned unsuccessfully for a seat in the provincial legislature.

It was another routine business trip to Toronto for Harold E. Wright, 57, of Vancouver. Well, almost routine. This time his colleagues at Canadian Bakeries Limited in Toronto would be congratulating him on being made a vice-president. The news was not public yet, but the boys would know. A busy five-day trip, and he would be back with lots of time to get things ready for Christmas.

Alderman Wally Rowan, a TCA employee, was heading home to Calgary with his wife and two children, and Mrs. E. L. Welch, whose daughter Judy had recently been chosen Miss Toronto, was looking forward to getting home to Scarborough, Ontario. Six of the passengers were Americans, five Chinese, and one, Hatsuko Hashimoto Dong, came from Osaka, in Japan.

Great mystery and many rumours were later to be attached to one of the Chinese, Kwan Song of New York City. He had been on a business trip to the Orient, and, according to a claim filed later, had a money-belt on him containing about $80,000 in cash. At any rate he had it when he left New York on the way to China. Whether he had any of it left when he was returning home nobody will ever know now. But when word of the possibility leaked out, police had to keep back hordes of people who wanted to risk their necks to look for it.

With this load, fascinating but to him routine, Captain Clark rolled down the runway in the dark and the rain. At 6.10 p.m. he was airborne, and the gloomy grey waters of Georgia Strait, laced with occasional white, were beneath him. As they climbed through the murky night, Terry Boon was reading off the long check-list that ensures that the pilot specifically examines every one of an astonishing number of dials, switches, and levers.

Because of the rough weather and the turbulence in the mountains east of Vancouver, Captain Clark had been advised to make his climb to the west, over open water. He did this now, spiralling up in wide, sweeping turns about ten miles south of the airport. As he climbed, he heard the voice of his friend Captain Jack Wright, who was just approaching Vancouver in Flight 7, a Super-Constellation.

Wright said he had run into head winds of ninety knots all the way across the Cascades. Rime ice up to an inch thick had formed on his wings, but had caused no serious trouble. "If I was going back, I'd fly at 19,000 or 20,000 feet," he told Clark.

Flight 810's pilot thanked him, and requested clearance to fly at 19,000 feet to Calgary. At 6.30 p.m. he started up the Fraser Valley, just a mile or so north of the U.S. border and parallel with it. He was at 12,500 feet, and estimated that he would reach Princeton at 6.58. It was slow work climbing with the heavily laden aircraft. At take-off, with the extra gas load for possible diversion because of bad weather, the CF-TFD weighed over thirty-eight tons. This was about one and a half tons below the permitted maximum.

At 6.40 p.m. he was over Cultus Lake, fifty-six miles east of the airport, and reported he was leaving 15,000 feet and going higher. Cultus is the start of the "Graveyard" at the base of the Cascades wall that soars to 8,000 feet and churns the oceans of air into violent currents. Flight 810 ran into them now. At 16,000 feet the pilots, looking out into an eerie, grey-encompassed world, saw that a coat of ice was already forming on their wings. The electric de-icers were working on it, however, and there was no great problem. The passengers knew nothing of this. Some of them, however, the ones who had not flown very often, felt queasy as the North Star bucked a little in the rough air. Clark reported matter-of-factly that this was "light to moderate turbulence".

It became a little rougher, and at 6.46 Clark told his company's radio dispatcher that they had run into "several jolts", which he guessed were caused by running through the tops of cumulus clouds merged in the general cloud mass. At 19,000 feet, the level at which he had been cleared to fly, he ran into some "real good jolts", he said over the radio. He was still in the clouds, and it was far too bumpy for the comfort of his passengers. So he asked the TCA dispatcher to clear with Air Traffic Control for flight at 21,000 feet.

Altitudes of air liners are rigidly controlled to minimize the danger of collision when they are flying at night or in bad weather. Heading east they fly at odd thousands of feet, which was the reason Clark asked now for 21,000 feet instead of 20,000. Heading west, they fly at even thousands, so that in poor visibility there is always a 1,000-foot vertical separation between planes that might be approaching each other head-on. As each one leaves a given altitude to go up or down, it must report to the Air Traffic Control Centre, which plots all movements carefully. Accordingly, Captain Clark was ordered at 6.49 p.m. to report when he was leaving 20,000 feet.

He never reached that altitude. Three minutes later, at 6.52, the receiver at TCA's operations office crackled with a message that started the whole sad train of tragedy. Clark's voice, calm and unhurried, said, "Looks like we had a fire in No. 2 engine."

He was then at 19,500 feet, and reported that he had immediately shut down the engine — the inboard one on the left side. There was much confusion about this later. Company officials said that Clark had merely reported that a fire-warning light came on, which may or may not have indicated there was a fire. Careful study of the recordings

71

made of the radio transmissions shows clearly that Clark said "had a fire" and did not mention the warning light. He did not mention the fire again, however, so it is presumed that the fire-fighting system, which works at the push of a button, did its job efficiently.

TCA told him to transfer to the Air Traffic Control frequency, which he did at once. He turned around and headed back towards Vancouver. Here is part of the official log of the next few vital minutes.

6.57 P.M. FLIGHT 810: Vancouver Centre, this is Flight 810. We have just lost No. 2 engine. We're holding 19,000 feet. We're endeavouring to maintain 19,000 feet. We would like a clearance immediately to get down if we can. We're losing altitude quite fast here.

FLIGHT 810: Confirm Flight 4 is holding 14,000 feet?

FLIGHT 810: And is that via Cultus Lake? [airway Red 44, which he had followed out]

VANCOUVER CENTRE: Via Green One [just north of Red 44], and you should be past Flight 4 shortly. He's coming up on Hope at the present, maintaining 14,000 feet via Green One.

FLIGHT 810: Maintain 14,000 feet. We are cleared to descend, then go ahead again.

VANCOUVER CENTRE: Maintain 14,000 feet.

FLIGHT 810: Confirm Flight 4 is holding 14,000 feet?

VANCOUVER CENTRE: Flight 4 is holding 13,000 feet.

FLIGHT 810: Thank you. We are leaving 19,000 feet at 6.57 on Green One.

VANCOUVER CENTRE: Okay, and report by Hope on this frequency.

FLIGHT 810: Roger, wilco [will comply].

The controller had cleared Clark down at once to 14,000 feet, though there was no alarm. A North Star, fully loaded, should be able not only to hold its height at that elevation, but to climb at about 300 feet a minute with one engine dead.

At 6.57, five minutes after the fire call, there was still no tension noticeable anywhere. At ATC it was still more or less routine. Air liners do not lose an engine every day but it is quite a common occurrence. Pilots practise regularly to cope with it.

At 7.01, Flight 4 reported: "Just passing Hope, 13,000 feet." ATC replied: "By Hope 7.01 at 13,000 feet, and Flight 810, what's your estimate on Hope?"

Flight 810: "Another five minutes, roughly, I believe."

Then ATC asked Captain Clark if he thought he could stay at 14,000 feet without trouble. "I think so," came the calm reply.

Captain Chester Rickard on Flight 4 heard the interchange, and came on the air with his own on-the-spot report of conditions. He told Clark: "Flight conditions are poor down here. We are running into strong subsidence and moderate icing between 11,000 and 13,000 feet. Maintain as much altitude as you can."

Clark told him he was almost down to 15,000 feet, and would maintain that height. The voice that came through the storm to the listening ears of Captain Rickard and First Officer David Moir sounded alert and quite relaxed. There was no hint in it of serious trouble, and the tone in which the brief words were said implied that Clark expected no difficulty in holding 15,000 feet.

However, he had obviously been a little bothered by the nearness of Flight 4, which was only a few minutes' flying time away and heading right towards him. As he himself was losing height quite quickly, and could not tell exactly where Flight 4 was, he apparently kept a little left to give Rickard plenty of room to pass.

Unseen and unheard, Flight 4 did pass safely, and a few minutes later reported it was "by Princeton". Rickard asked clearance to climb to 15,000 feet, but ATC could not raise him to give the necessary approval. At 7.08, Captain Clark, seemingly unruffled, was able to relay the approval to Flight 4. At this time, Clark told Rickard, it was snowing, and he didn't know "if it looked good or not".

The radio log continues the story:

7.10 P.M. FLIGHT 810: 810 by Hope, request descent down to 10,000 feet.

VANCOUVER CENTRE: Roger, 810 now cleared Vancouver Range Station, cross Vancouver 8,000 feet or above, and remain this frequency.

FLIGHT 810: Roger, Range, cross 8,000 feet or above. Will remain.

With this normal, routine acknowledgment, Captain Clark and his sixty-one companions vanished for ever from the face of the earth.

Down at Birch Bay, Washington, an operator at a United States military radar station was following the course of a "blip" on his screen. He had seen it on the way out, and reported it to Canadian radar headquarters, which took over responsibility for watching it.

Now, however, it had turned around at a place where planes on this route normally did not turn around. His interest was aroused, and he began to plot its progress. Each twelve seconds a beam of light swept around the radarscope and struck the tiny "blip" that represented an air liner and sixty-two people. Each time the position changed slightly, and was marked down.

At 7.11 p.m. the plot placed Flight 810 about twenty-one miles south-east of Hope, and twelve miles south of the southern boundary of Airway Green One – yet he was in the region of another airway, over higher peaks, where the minimum safety altitude specified was 9,600 feet.

There was no way for the radar operator to know all this detail, however. So when the blip did not show up twelve seconds later, he was not particularly worried. Radar signals are "line of sight", which means an aircraft behind a big mountain is invisible to radar, as it would be to the human eye. Mountainous terrain causes many blind spots, and aircraft regularly fade from the radarscopes. This one faded near Silvertip Mountain, 8,500 feet high, about twenty-one miles north of Slesse.

The Air Traffic Control Centre waited a few minutes after Captain Clark's acknowledgment. When they heard nothing more, they called him at 7.21 with instructions for landing at Vancouver. His estimated time of arrival was 7.40 and fire trucks and crash crews were already standing by in case of trouble on the landing. He did not answer. Everyone in the control room suddenly tensed, and the next messages that went out every few minutes were urgent. Still no answer. A call went through at 7.22 to the Royal Canadian Air Force's Rescue Co-ordination Centre, which is on a private direct line. Crews were called and stood ready with their aircraft, while ATC kept calling to Flight 810.

It was 11.15 p.m. before TCA officially reported the air liner was considered overdue. By that time, a dramatic and dangerous air search

74

was already under way, despite the appalling weather. At 8.36 p.m. an RCAF CF-100 jet interceptor, already flying on night exercises, was diverted to the scene. Another was "scrambled" from its base, and the pair searched as much of the area as the clouds permitted. These aircraft were then Canada's principal air defenders, equipped to operate in the worst weather. There was really very little that could be done by other search planes under the conditions, but at 10.52 Flight Lieutenant Phil Walker took off in a Dakota (DC-3) from the RCAF's 121 Communications and Rescue Flight. Flying Officer R. C. Tomlinson took up another twenty-five minutes later. Flying Officer George Waugh, veteran of many searches, was up by 11.55, and a four-engined Lancaster used for coast patrol joined the hunt within half an hour.

All the pilots reported the weather was "atrocious", with winds aloft of more than ninety m.p.h., severe buffeting, and heavy icing on their aircraft. For three hours they flew above and through the storm, following the probable track of Flight 810, and looking vainly for lights or fires that might lead them to the place where CF-TFD was down.

Before dawn the briefing-room at 121 Flight was jammed with searchers. Squadron Leader George Sheahan, the search-master, told them: "There are three possibilities. First, that the plane became lost after radio failure. Second, that the pilot lost control completely. Third, that the aircraft blew up. All we have to go on at the moment is conjecture, but there is more to this than meets the eye because the pilot was doing everything he should have done.

"This is going to be tough searching weather. Try the peaks first and get down within 100 or 200 feet of the ground you are searching. But for God's sake be careful."

As soon as it was light enough to see, the aircraft roared off. Seventeen were in the air within a few minutes of daylight, with the hopeless task of covering 4,800 square miles of cloud-smothered mountains where the plane could be. Ten doctors stood by at the airport to handle survivors. One plane waited with medical men ready to parachute to the scene of the crash, and the giant Piasecki helicopter was placed strategically up the Fraser Valley. This machine has several times been able to lift wrecked light aircraft from mountain peaks, and has tremendous possibilities.

It was not long before Squadron Leader Sheahan's warning about the weather was borne out. Over the radio at 121 H.Q. came a pilot's voice asking, "How are the other crews? Mine are all sick." He soon found that the other crews, shaken unmercifully as strapped-in pilots tried to manoeuvre in the valleys, were all the same. Sheahan reported, "Planes are being just about turned onto their backs." Flying Officer H. S. Gamblin, navigator of a Dakota, was knocked almost unconscious when hurled from his seat. Another member of the same crew said, "We were thrown around so much that straps were breaking and our safety equipment was flying all over the place. I've never seen turbulence like it before."

Another aircraft returned to base briefly because flares and other explosive pyrotechnics had come loose and were being hurled around inside. The pilot was afraid that one of them might ignite and cause disaster to his own aircraft.

All that day and Tuesday the weather stayed bad. On the Wednesday it was so bad that nobody even attempted to get into the air. More than sixty aircraft stood impotently on the ground. Over 500 would-be rescuers, including pilots, parachutists, mountaineers, doctors, and nurses, waited in helpless groups, praying for a break in the weather. Already more than a foot of new snow had fallen above the 3,000-foot level, the weatherman estimated. Nobody knew for sure just how much, because the clouds would not lift high enough for a check.

But if the fliers were helpless, there was still lots of work to be done. Possible leads came flooding in from all directions. Everybody seemed to have heard explosions in the mountains and aeroplanes thundering low overhead. Many of the reports were simply fantastic, and to take them all in meant covering an area of 7,800 square miles, almost all of it mountainous. Police and airmen toured the Fraser Valley, speaking to everyone who claimed to have heard something.

Gradually, from the welter of confusion, a pattern began to appear. Slowly, the heart of the search area was defined: a block of tall mountains fifty miles long and thirty miles wide, on either side of a line stretching from Hope south-west to Chilliwack, a farming town sixty miles from Vancouver.

The investigators plotted on maps the reports they checked and found that the credible ones divided themselves into two groups. One group pointed to the area of Silvertip, a steep and pointed peak of

8,500 feet thirty-five miles east of Chilliwack. The other indicated Mount Slesse, a vicious-looking, rarely-climbed spire of rock just eighteen miles south-east of Chilliwack. But the clouds had been so low and the wind so strong when the North Star vanished that pin-pointing was impossible. Cloud and wind had diffused the light and sound over a vast area.

One of those whose reports supported the Silvertip region was Gordon Dowding, a member of the Legislative Assembly. He was dining at a lodge on the summit of the Hope-Princeton Highway when six excited people rushed in and reported an "explosion like an atomic bomb". Minutes later three more came in with the same report. All said it came from the Silvertip area, which is fifteen miles west of the lodge but within six miles of the highway. There is no doubt that the explosion they saw was the crash, though it came from more than thirty miles away.

Corporal Melford Henwood, a 27-year-old soldier stationed at Chilliwack, was alone in his car on a rough road about five miles west of Chilliwack, looking for some good ground to ski on during the coming winter. He told police that between 7.20 and 8 p.m. suddenly he saw "the most beautiful flash of light I've ever seen. It was a twirling mass of colours . . . very pretty colours. It twirled down towards the mountain and then shot up into the air for about 500 feet. I could see red light flickering."

Henwood scrambled from his car and sat on the hood, trying to make a sketch of the scene by the light, which was "almost as plain as day". Then, he said, "there was this explosion. It almost blew me off the hood."

Tying in closely with this was a report from a hunter, Jean Voight, also of Chilliwack. He was at Ryder Lake, five miles east of the town, when he saw a "mushroom flash, pink to orange in colour, and about 20 miles away". He promptly drove a stake into the ground and took a compass bearing on the flash. It was 110 degrees, or east-south-east.

This information, however, was not proving of very much help to the flying searchers. On Thursday, eighteen planes were in the air, trying vainly to pierce the layers of ice-filled clouds. By 10.30 a.m. all had been recalled. On the ground there was furious activity. The network of rough logging roads that lace the heart of the search area was being checked and checked again by men in trucks, in jeeps, on foot, and on horseback. Many of the men carried binoculars and scanned the thick forest on the slopes for some helpful sign. They found none. There was no road from which the crash site could be seen.

At the week-end, mountaineers began climbing the slopes of Silvertip and the near-by mountains. I was one of them, and even on snowshoes I sank to my waist in powder snow at the higher levels. It was futile, back-breaking work, with little chance of seeing anything beyond a hundred feet in the cloud. A party of loggers climbed part-way up a ridge north of Silvertip and came back with reports of hoarse cries for help coming from above them in the mist. They could go no higher because of the danger of avalanching snow. It sounded to us as if they had heard the raucous cry of a raven, but another party was sent in next day to investigate. Nothing was found.

The second week of the search opened on Monday, December 17, with the entire area still buried by cloud, rain, and snow. For the first time TCA's president, G. R. McGregor, admitted that "little hope can be entertained for the survival of the people aboard". The Queen carried the presumption a little farther. Her message said: "I have heard with deep concern of the tragic loss of the Canadian air liner in the Rocky Mountains. Please convey my sincere sympathy to all relatives of those who lost their lives."

It was December 19 before any sizeable air search could take place, but by then it was too late. Deep new snow blanketed all the peaks and the chances of finding even the giant, intact tail-section of the North Star were infinitesimal. The rainfall at Chilliwack for December, and the consequent snow-fall at higher levels, was twice the normal average for the month. Rarely could planes find a clear hour or two, and, when they did, Squadron Leader Sheahan rushed his best men into the area. Finally, on December 27, after a sad, uncertain Christmas for the relatives, the search was curtailed.

Henceforth, said Sheahan, there would be good-weather searching only. "There is no hope of survivors as far as we are concerned. The sense of urgency in the search has now gone. We don't intend searching in weather that can endanger search crews."

The mountains had won this round. The obliterating blanket of white that hides a million blemishes on the face of nature was thickening steadily. There was no chance of finding the plane before the summer thaw. It might even turn out to be another case like the mysterious disaster that hit a TCA Lodestar air liner on April 29, 1947. There were fifteen people aboard, and Captain W. G. Pike asked Vancouver control for permission to land. He was asked to make another circuit, and agreed. He was never heard from again. The wreckage of his plane was never found.

Or would searchers have better luck, as they did in 1943? On December 20, 1942, a Canadian Pacific Airlines plane vanished in similar fashion when almost at Vancouver. It carried thirteen people. It was found on August 17, 1943, when a team led by Charles Woodsworth, city editor of the *Vancouver Province,* reached the scene at the top of Mount William Knight. This was only ten miles from, and within sight of, Mount Slesse.

When the active search for the North Star was curtailed, Sheahan and his experts went once again through the "dream file", which consisted of letters from well-intentioned people all over the world. Nothing had come from studying them in the first anxious days of the search, but now in desperation they were examined again. They were really fine examples of the astonishing twists that can be taken by the devious human mind.

Many of the writers "knew" just where the plane was lying. They based their knowledge, which was certain in their own minds, on many abstruse factors, many of which were variations of the divining-rod technique used in hunts for water. A forked stick properly held over the map, said the would-be helpers, would twitch to show the location of the wreck. Some people sent in the results of the readings from tea-leaves in the bottom of their cups. One map received from South Africa had carefully marked on it places where the sender said pieces of the aircraft lay.

Somebody else "knew" the North Star was at the bottom of a lake hundreds of miles away in Alberta. He sent in a complete set of engineering drawings to back up his theory, and for good measure provided plans of a special hoist to lift the plane to the surface.

One 69-year-old man from Vancouver Island was confident that he could "get on the beam" and find the missing plane in from five minutes to half an hour. His technique was known as "radiesthesie", a variation of extra-sensory perception. All his method needed in the way of search equipment, he said, was a pendulum, a piece of copper wire, a map, and something identified with the object for which he was looking. Finally, there were correspondents who relied on old-fashioned methods. They knew the plane was in such-and-such a spot because they had simply dreamed about it.

During January and February, however, a scientifically much sounder method was being used as a last-ditch effort to find the plane before a score of feet of snow buried it for months — and perhaps for ever. With a special technique of aerial photography, Aero Surveys Limited covered about 750 square miles in perfect weather. The photographs, taken from about 12,000 feet, have a fifty-per-cent over-lap, and can be placed under a stereoscope to give a three-dimensional picture. The technique has been used with great success to measure the amount of timber in a given area, to find spots of blight infestation in forest areas, and to pick out many things that the human eye cannot see. In this case, however, the eye of the camera was baffled too.

The weeks slipped by, and gradually all those who had been involved in the giant search went back to their routine way of life. There were several false alarms. Planes flying on routine trips reported shiny objects in the snow below; men in the valleys saw metallic glittering on the mountains above. Searching planes always took to the air at once, but all the objects proved to be innocent.

On Thursday, May 9, five months to the day after the disappearance, TCA's regional operations manager Norman Donnelly called a meeting to plan the resumption of the search. Already the snow was melting away at lower levels, and the first vague chances of finding the wreck might appear within a few weeks. Present at the meeting were officials of TCA, the RCAF, Canada's Department of Transport, the Mountain Rescue Group, Okanagan Helicopters Limited, the Royal Canadian Mounted Police, and Aero Surveys.

It was decided that the RCAF would soon resume regular searches, with up to a dozen aircraft at a time. The mountaineers would make weekly checks of the snow depth. As soon as they thought it feasible, a photo-survey of more than 2,000 square miles would be made. During the weekend of June 1-2, the RCAF helicopter would drop a score of mountaineers at picked viewpoints on alpine ridges throughout the area. With well-steadied binoculars, they could search the area almost tree by tree. Even then, however, there was a good chance of missing such tiny flecks in the awesome face of nature. In 1954, I was one of a party that found the wreck of an RCAF plane on Mount Arrowsmith, on Vancouver Island. We landed high on the peak by jumping from a hovering helicopter. Then Ulf Bitterlich noticed a wavy line in the snow, which seemed to him to be out of place in the gaunt, right-angled world of rock. We had trouble pin-pointing the line he meant; so he used four rocks in the snow, which were roughly in the shape of a diamond, to act as markers in directing our gaze. We all looked at them through binoculars, and then followed the line to the suspicious wavy line in the snow. Two of the party set off towards it, and I sat down to rest the binoculars on a boulder for a more careful look. Then the "rocks" that made up the diamond showed up as parts of the wreck, covered with an inch or two of frost and snow. When a helicopter came over a few minutes later, it hovered within thirty feet of the pieces, but the crew could not see them.

Despite such difficulties in mountain searching, however, the meeting that planned the new hunt for the North Star broke up in an atmosphere of confidence.

Said Donnelly, "I have every reason to believe the new search will be successful." Sheahan commented, "If it is in pieces big enough to find, we'll find it."

As it turned out, all this expensive organization was never to be used.

Just two days later, Elfrida Pigou and her friends lost their way in the clouds and took the wrong route up Mount Slesse. The first mystery, at least, of Canada's most baffling air disaster was solved.

The first clue, however, simply opened the door for a thousand new and urgent problems. Donnelly asked me if I would, on behalf of TCA, fly immediately to the Slesse area by helicopter and assess the situation as a mountaineer. Where was the rest of the wreck? Could we reach it? Could bodies and parts of the plane be removed? A helicopter stood by a few yards away and the pilot, Evan Bullock, had his own briefing. How close could a helicopter get? Where was the best place to set up a base camp near the mountain?

Soon after 11 a.m. we took off in his Bell G-47, which resembles nothing so much as a flying bubble. Shortly afterwards, we were able to pick up the climbing party's tracks in the snow as they wound upwards.

It was an eerie feeling, using a machine like this magic bubble to follow tiny steps towards the clouds. The peaks were still shrouded, and as we skirted underneath the cloud, light snow was falling from it. Long before it reached the ground it turned into rain. Thanks to Elfrida Pigou's directions and map, it was easy to follow her party's route. We landed twice, once on the east side and once on the west. Carefully we searched both mountain flanks through binoculars.

When I casually write "landed" now, it sounds like a simple operation, but it was a revelation to watch the way Bullock set his craft down on the steep slopes. Each time he picked out a knoll on top of a cliff and set it down lightly as a feather. Take-off was breath-taking. He simply revved up the motor until the helicopter was just airborne, then hurled it down the precipice. This is to build up forward speed, but the first time you try it, it is far more likely to build up a heart attack.

Our binocular searching showed nothing, although, as we found the next day, the eastern landing-spot, at 5,300 feet, was just about on top of some of the wreckage, which was concealed by deep snow.

Now the cloud was lifting, and we went up towards the place where Elfrida had found the big piece of aluminum. So far, we had been able to search only the lower levels. The climbers' finds had all been on the west side of the ridge, but now we could search both sides of the pinnacle, gradually climbing higher. At last, on the east side, at about 7,400 feet, Bullock's eyes, sharpened by years of hunting coyotes from the air for game departments, spotted a piece of red-streaked paper on the rocks. It could have been a sandwich-wrapping from yesterday's climbing party, but we didn't really think so.

Less than two hundred feet above, we found it at last. Bullock went so close that I felt sure his whirling rotor would clip the snow from the ledges. Now we could see a tangle of snow-covered pieces resting on a small ledge. Above the ledge was a thirty-foot wall of naked rock. And fifty feet above the top of that was the open air that Flight 810 had needed to avert disaster.

From our airborne perch, we could see the serenity of the little hamlets in the Fraser Valley. But the spot, so near them, where sixty-two people had died was a place of stark and savage wilderness.

The only movement we could see was the birth of an avalanche, as it began its slide to the valley below, and the anguished writhing of clouds among the spire-like peaks. A hundred feet to the right and the North Star might have gone through the gap in the ridge. A hundred feet above and it would have cleared the terrible teeth of the mountain.

A couple of miles away, though, and right across its route, was a twin ridge, the Border Peaks, that would almost certainly have finished the job had Slesse fumbled.

Quickly we returned and got ready for an attempt to reach the two key spots the next day, May 14. Eight members of the Mountain Rescue Group took part. Miss Pigou came to the 7,600-foot impact site with Waldemar (Fips) Broda, Jack Russell, and me. We planned to reach the site by climbing the west slope, crossing the summit ridge, and descending to the crash site.

Another party went to the snow-slopes on the east side, where wreckage would have landed after a fall of more than 2,000 feet down a vertical cliff beneath the point of impact. This party consisted of Roy Mason, Ian Kay, Joseph Hutton, and Russell Yard.

We landed on the west-side knoll at 5,700 feet, with Bullock touching down in the same three-inch-wide skid-marks he had made in the snow there the day before. Climbing on this side was not too difficult — the hardest stretches were about Grade Four of a classification standard that reaches Grade Six. We carried with us an RCMP portable radio with which we were to report what we found. When we reached the place where Dave Cathcart had rested, we tried to call the base below. All we could get on our trackless mountain was a list of cars stolen on the highways far below. Call as we would, we got no answer.

Soon we were up to the highest point reached by the earlier party, and we knew that on the east face, right below us, the wreckage lay. The face was steep, but after a quick look at it we decided not to use climbing-ropes. The whole area was composed of rotten rocks, so loose that the touch of a climbing-rope would have knocked many pieces off. And there was no secure spot where one man could anchor and safely let the other down. Slowly, cautiously, we moved around loose blocks, sliding down through a hole at the back of one.

Now, suddenly, we started to see fragments of metal around us. I was ahead as we went around one big corner. Just a few feet above my head a sizeable piece of wreckage swung against the vertical rock, held by a thin control cable that had accidentally looped around a flake of rock. In the wreckage was part of a body, and I warned the others. Elfrida, her job well done, moved a few feet to one side. "You men were all in the war," she said quietly. "You are more accustomed to

83

this sort of thing than I am. I don't want to go any farther."

We examined this piece of wreckage carefully, crawling between it and the rock face. We felt it might be technically possible to remove it, but very hazardous, as any interference would probably dislodge the entire mass. Just a few feet below the steep slope quickened, and curved out of sight, dropping vertically for more than 2,000 feet to the snow-field. Anybody trying to retrieve this fragment of a body might easily wind up there too.

As we wound through the wreckage, I knocked off a rock the size of a baseball. It landed on Fips Broda's head, but he was so close that though it hurt him it did no harm. We squeezed our way along the cliff face, taking photographs as we went. A few minutes later, we were in the saucer-shaped depression where the plane had hit.

The destruction was absolute. One of the finest, most luxurious creations of man, a world in miniature, had turned in a second to ruins. A little girl's dress lay crumpled on a rock, A pair of ear-rings gleamed brightly, still fixed to their show-card. A half-burned, high-heeled shoe, some coins, a dozen paper cups, and parts of a newspaper were scattered forlornly through the maze of metal. Much of it was mercifully covered with a foot of snow, but here and there we could see fragmentary human remains which showed the shattering force with which the impact came.

Russell, Broda, and I moved across the wreckage, leaving Elfrida out of sight below. Jack lightly touched a strip of metal as he went through. It touched another, which moved an inch and levered off a heavy boulder poised on the edge of a drop. Suddenly the peace and quiet of this remote spot was shattered and our heads were ringing with infernal noise.

The rock bounded evilly down, clattering on wreckage as it went, and in a second the precipices rang with the shrieks of falling metal. The noise of hell itself roared all around us.

But worse, Elfrida was out of sight below, in the path of the avalanching debris. We shouted vainly to her, our voices swamped in the flood of echoes that seemed to make the mountain shake. For minutes we waited, while the echoing roars died down.

Finally, we heard her tiny voice. Our first warning shout had reached her, and her instant reflex had sent her diving beneath an overhanging shelf of rock.

84

MOUNT LOGAN

The monumental massif of Mount Logan (19,850 feet) is a range in itself,
and Canada's highest summit. It is west of Whitehorse, in one of the
world's most heavily glaciated regions. Photo 1 shows the fluted south-east
ridge, looking south-west to Mount St. Elias. The first climbers (in 1925)
followed Logan Glacier (photo 2); they turned right on the glacier
beneath the summit. (*Photos by Bradford Washburn*)

1

MOUNT WADDINGTON

This 13,177-foot peak, Canada's highest outside the Yukon, was discovered in 1925. Tiedemann Glacier (photo 3, foreground) is now the standard approach. The summit spire (photo 4) was not climbed until 1936. Giant "ice-feathers" are a constant menace. Behind the climbers near Bravo Col (photo 5) is Mount Munday, named for the couple who found the peak. *(Photos 3 and 5 by Byron Olson, photo 4 by Mrs. Phyl Munday)*

3

4

MOUNT SLESSE

Almost through this granite gap, a TCA North Star crashed on Mount Slesse in 1956. Sixty-two died. Photo 6 shows the gap and the wreckage on the face of the precipice. Photo 7 shows how control cables held the wreckage dangling above a drop of 2,000 feet on the 8,200-foot peak. *(Photos by Paddy Sherman)*

MOUNT ROBSON

The most famous of Canada's mountains is this difficult and dangerous
crest of the Rockies, 12,972 feet high. Photo 8 shows the approach from the
east. Climbers hack their way up cliffs of snow and ice near the summit
(photo 9). An unstable snow cornice hangs from the south-east shoulder
(photo 10); at the left, above the bubbling clouds, is Mount Resplendent.
(Photos by Ed Cooper)

9

MOUNT SEYMOUR

Even small peaks must be treated with
respect. Mount Seymour (4,758 feet) is
in Vancouver's backyard (photo 12),
yet Alick Patterson was trapped there
for six days before being rescued (photo
11). *(Photo 12 by Charles Jones, photo
11 by William Howice)*

11

12

MOUNT FAIRWEATHER

Clouds cover the Gulf of Alaska below tiny High Camp (photo 13). Climbers thread through ice towers (photo 14), camp on crevassed glaciers (photo 16), and "swim" dangerous crevasses (photo 17). The view from Lituya Bay (photo 15) shows how tidal waves have stripped shorelines bare of trees. *(Photos 13, 14, and 16 by Fips Broda, photo 15 by Bradford Washburn, photo 17 by Paddy Sherman)*

It was a warning of what would come if any serious effort was made to disturb the wreckage. Quietly and carefully we searched on now. Nuts and bolts clung to the near-vertical walls of rock, held there by the adhesive weight of winter snow, ready now to fall at the slightest breath of wind. Part of an instrument panel was hidden in a crack amid the rocks. Three or four of the instruments had stayed in the frame, but the hands had snapped off under the impact, and they told nothing of the fatal story. We picked up mail and a purse and moved back to safety at the top of the ridge.

There we sat, as planes and helicopters buzzed close with official photographers, and discussed our views on the situation. It was unanimous — indeed to experienced climbers there was no alternative. Had someone been injured at the impact site, there would be no hesitation in trying to rescue him. It would be an extremely dangerous task, but with a life at stake nobody would quibble at danger. For fragmentary remains, however, such risks were not justifiable. After the summer thaw, the slopes at the foot of the cliffs would yield most of the debris, and some of this could be reached without hazard.

We could see the other party at our feet now — Mason, Kay, Hutton, and Yard — moving like insects 2,000 feet below, between the threads of big crevasses. They heard our shouts, and diminutive arms were raised in reply.

Later, back at Chilliwack, Roy Mason told us: "The crevasses ranged from ten to perhaps seventy feet deep, and there was considerable movement of the snow. There were many small avalanches and several times the overhanging lips of crevasses cracked and tumbled in. We saw no signs of bodies. But about ten to fifteen feet down in the walls of the crevasses we could see a layer of debris, including clothing, luggage and aircraft parts."

It was not feasible then to try to recover anything from the crevasses, he said. Chances would be better in the late summer, but it might never be feasible. The snow, almost a glacier, was resting on steep slabs and was in constant, stirring motion that could tend to bury the debris even deeper. Just a few yards away the slabs steepened again to a cliff. This could slide the ruins another thousand feet down to a bush-knit tangle of rock.

Mason and I gave evidence that night when Coroner Glen McDonald opened his grim inquiry. We warned of the danger to life involved

85

in any meddling with the wreckage, and said that later in the year much of the hazard would disappear, at least at the lower site. Coroner McDonald suggested that importing crack mountain-rescue men from Europe might be the answer. The next day, Search-master Sheahan was quoted on similar lines. "This is a multi-million-dollar operation," he said, "and there is no sense relying on local opinions when we can get the best available anywhere within forty-eight hours."

Broda, our most experienced man, soon disposed of these glamorous suggestions. He testified on May 15: "I come from Austria and I have been in the mountain guide school. I served with the mountain group during the war, training mountaineering troops, and from 1943 I was with the mountain rescue group in Austria for seven years until coming here. I know the local climbers quite well. In my opinion, for rescue work they are just as good as those we knew over at home."

Climbing to the impact site was not too difficult, he said, but "very, very dangerous" because of conditions over which the climber could have no control.

He summed up: "It is an unwritten law that you should never endanger human lives for parts of bodies and fragments. If there is a chance to get someone out still half alive, we do set our lives at stake. But not for pieces and fragments of bodies."

Several incidents showed the wisdom of Broda's judgment. That very afternoon, RCAF Sergeant "Buzz" Sawyer had been on the lower slopes with David Quigley, the coroner's mortuary attendant. They had gone to see what possibility there was of removing a body from a crevasse. Nobody told the mountaineers they were going, and a helicopter landed them at 5,300 feet. As they were looking around on comparatively easy terrain, a thirty-foot vertical wall of snow collapsed with a roar near by. "We had to move fast to get out of there," said Quigley. Sawyer suggested that the whole area was so dangerous that it should be placed out of bounds to everybody.

So the hearing was closed indefinitely, and the area was banned to all hikers and aircraft under heavy penalties. Even being found within half a mile was made a punishable offence, while touching the wreckage carried a penalty of five thousand dollars and a year in jail.

From the day after the North Star vanished, another investigation had also been under way, carried out by a three-man board from the Department of Transport, the federal body in charge of regulating aviation. It was headed by Desmond D. Murphy, a slight, wiry man of fifty-six, who had been a celebrated test pilot and had done much of the test flying on the first North Star. He was a perfectionist, and, though he had never climbed a mountain in his life, he felt it was his duty to reach the remote and dangerous impact site at 7,600 feet.

Somebody had to make a technical examination at the site, he felt, and it was too dangerous to assign anybody. So he asked us to take him, although his family and superiors tried hard to dissuade him. First, we said, he had to get into training. First thing each morning he drove from his home to Grouse Mountain, on the North Shore, and hiked up the steep track used by a chair-lift. He would climb about 1,600 feet, and then carry on to work. Finally we felt he was ready.

On June 25 Broda and I took him up Mount Slesse. On the earlier trips to the peak, we had used a tiny Bell helicopter. It just fitted neatly on the snow-covered knoll. This time we went in the RCAF's giant Vertol, which just dwarfed the landing-spot. By some brilliant flying, Flight Lieutenant Pat Mathews put one wheel down and held the machine steady while we leaped out.

Then, with a deafening roar, he was away. Desmond Murphy, a flier by nature and training, was on his own two feet to climb the first real mountain in his life. He did astonishingly well. Broda went first, and with infinite kindness and care prepared the way. He kicked solid steps in the snow, and we safeguarded with axe and rope Murphy's every move. The going steepened, switched to rock. A vertical wall, with an awkward move in the middle. Broda helped above, I helped below, and Murphy went neatly up. Far from being scared, he became mildly exhilarated as the valley dropped away below him.

Over the crest we went, slowly, and down onto the shattered face. Despite the danger of knocking down rocks with the rope, we left it on to safeguard him as best we could and moved with exaggerated caution.

For a man's first time on a mountain, the situation was frighteningly impressive. The eye moved spellbound through the debris speckling the rotten rocks, lingered on the steepening curve of cliff, and then plunged irresistibly 2,000 feet down through space. Murphy told the resumed inquiry later: "It is a somewhat hair-raising experience to be up on that mountain."

To the north and south, the vertical lines of rock showed what the unseen cliff was like below us: hopeless for climbing, and always exposed to the lethal fire of rocks from above.

We moved through the debris, while Murphy, veteran of many accident investigations, shook his head in wonder at the absolute destruction. On the shoulder of the ledge where lay the main mass of wreckage, we unroped him and seated him in a safe spot. Everything here was unstable. Here was where Russell's merest touch had sent the boulder hurtling down. From this vantage point he could look over the jumble of wreckage, and direct us to move about seeking serial numbers and details of equipment.

On a rock about thirty feet away, a propeller lay at an almost impossible angle. Fips leaned gingerly over it from above, and delicately began to wipe off grease that hid the numbers on the hub. It suddenly slid towards the abyss. I had my back towards him at that moment, but Mr. Murphy testified later: "I thought it rather plucky of Mr. Broda; he grabbed the propeller by the blades on either side of the hub and by leaning back brought it to a stop by the friction of the metal on the rock."

We were moving as fast as we could because already the brief spell of clear weather was disintegrating before our eyes. Clouds were swallowing up the mountains only a few miles to the west and south, and wisps started drifting to us through the V-shaped saddle to the north, through which the North Star had so nearly scraped. So we hurried down. The descent was even more ticklish for an inexperienced man. His climb had taken seven hours, and he was getting very tired.

Already the valley below, up which the helicopter must make its way to pluck us off at the appointed time, was filling with cloud. It was boiling up towards us, and we were preparing to put up our tent for the night when we heard the motor. Again the masterly one-wheeled balance while we clambered furiously in, and the ungainly looking machine, nicknamed the "Flying Banana", was safely off.

To Murphy, it was obvious that the key, if it was ever to be found, lay in the snow 2,000 feet below the spot he had so laboriously reached. And the snow still lay thick, effectively shielding the answer. Only one thing was sure to his expert eye: the aircraft had not been flying straight and level when it hit. Such total demolition could have come only from impact at a very high speed – much faster than the plane could have flown on three engines against a terrific headwind.

It was late in August before he had the last chance to inspect the lower site. The Mountain Rescue Group had been watching snow conditions carefully, and finally these reached a stage where we felt it was now or never. At any time now, under the miserable weather that existed, new snow could fall at the higher levels of the mountain. Roy Mason and Arthur Dellow made a very tough ascent from the east through bush and cliffs to examine the lower site.

At last, they found, the mountain was reluctantly showing some of its secrets. Some of the slabs were bare. Above them walls of snow would totter and crash, and spill their contents over a wide area. Things that had been buried fifteen feet down were now exposed to view, and they photographed all they saw. It was obvious that none of the would-be looters, inspired by dreams of the $80,000 money belt, had reached the scene: in prominent spots lay small amounts of money in various denominations, just as they were deposited by the vanishing snow.

At once the final lap was on. Helicopters shuttled in the Coroner, Glen McDonald, Desmond Murphy, and Department of Transport and RCMP officials. Mr. Murphy's experts were able to identify many of the major parts of the aircraft as they moved about under the careful supervision of Roy Mason. On August 27 and 28, parts of seventeen bodies were recovered, none of them recognizable. All were buried, and a rough-hewn cross was made of branches from a lone tree growing near by.

Coroner McDonald read a simple Anglican service, and Corporal Thomas J. Anderson of the RCMP read a service in memory of the Roman Catholics.

Finally, on September 11, Staff Sergeant William Wallace and ten men, ferried in by helicopter, went through the area again and buried the remains of nine more. The rest, the mountain will hold secret for ever.

The men worked hard and quietly for more than an hour and a half. Then they moved to the helicopter landing-site. But Slesse was far from finished with men who would ignore her blind malevolence. Wallace said later, "We were out of there approximately five minutes when two large avalanches went right over where we had been working."

The Coroner's inquiry was able to reach a formal verdict: the sixty-two people aboard North Star CF-TFD died accidentally. But what caused the accident will never be known. The aeronautical detectives worked hard. They found enough major parts to deduce that the aircraft was whole when it hit — no wing had come off in flight, and there had been no pre-crash explosion, in spite of rumours to the contrary. Many seat-belts were found at the lower site. Few of them were buckled, indicating that there was no alarm, at least among the fifty-nine passengers, as they roared through the stormy night.

The disaster that befell them was instant and catastrophic. Neither of the pilots had time to use the radio. No saboteur's bomb had caused the crash — but it came with just the same lethal speed and finality.

The final government report said carefully: "There is a high probability that the aircraft, while flying on three engines, encountered either severe icing, turbulence, subsidence or a combination of all three, or suffered some other difficulty of such a sudden or dire nature that the crew were unable to communicate with any agency or control the aircraft."

In the twenty-one miles after reporting "by Hope" the air liner had lost 6,400 feet in height. Severe precipitation could have caused this, or loss of another engine, or subsidence. One or all of these brought it low enough, apparently, to put it within range of the fearsome eddies in the lee of Slesse.

One other major question went unanswered: why was Flight 810 not on Green Airway No. 1, to which it had been assigned by Air Traffic Control? Not only was careful, methodical Captain Clark far south of the southern limit of Green One, but he was also south of Red 44, which is some miles south of Green One. Why?

Captain Rickard, flying the Viscount that was so near the North Star when it vanished, told the government inquiry that from Chilliwack to a few miles east of Hope, the low-frequency-radio range signals were not always reliable. Storms and mountains play strange tricks with radio waves.

The report noted: "Under good reception conditions, both Vancouver and Princeton radio ranges are audible at the midway point between them (near Hope). Under the conditions that existed that evening, it is probable that radio reception on the range signals was zero in the Hope area, and positive fixing of position difficult, if not impossible.

"This is borne out by Capt. Rickard's recollection. This could contribute, and probably did, to Flight 810 crew's unawareness that they were so far south of Green One."

The beacon at Hope, which activates the radio-direction-finder needle when the aircraft goes "by Hope" within thirty miles or so, was also found to be unsatisfactory. The board recommended that it should be strengthened or re-positioned, although it was stressed that there was no evidence that this had helped to cause the accident.

There was no way to establish the answer clearly, the report said. But this, it suggested, was the probable one:

Captain Clark was worried about the Viscount fast approaching him. Normally the Viscount is a fast aircraft. With a tail wind of about 100 m.p.h., it would be making a tremendous ground speed. Clark was not sure that his iced-up North Star could keep enough height to be certain of staying above the Viscount. So, prudent and cautious as ever, he turned a little to the south to give Flight 4 absolutely safe passage.

When he had switched off the inboard engine on the port side, this would give greater thrust from the two engines on the starboard side, tending to turn the aircraft. Automatically he would compensate for this by trimming the controls, heading the aircraft a little crabwise to keep it flying a straight path. This would tend to make him drift even farther south.

Normally, this would not matter much, because he could tell from his radio range signals that he was drifting off-course and could correct for it.

But this night, in the terrific storm, his radio reception was so bad he could not make the correction. "It is reasoned," said the report, "that the crew of Flight 810 were aware they were south of Green One, but not of the extent of the departure. It is considered probable that more or less extensive interference to the reception of the LF radio ranges contributed."

All this is at best informed conjecture. One thing, however, is sure: the men and women whose lives ended here are locked in a sanctuary as proud as any on earth.

This is a place where I would gladly lie. The rock is clean and bereft of sadness, the deep quiet has a tranquillity all its own. At their heads, peaks reach for the sky in a sweep of stark grandeur, and the mountain itself is their monument.

The Dangerous
Mountain

MOUNT ROBSON

The argument began just as they had finished their breakfast at high camp and were ready to set off for the summit of Mount Robson. It was not a bad-tempered argument, for all six men were good friends who had climbed together on many peaks in North America. Now they had come from California to train for an attempt on Mount Makalu, giant neighbour of Mount Everest. They shared a tremendous amount of climbing knowledge among them, but no esoteric disagreement on technicalities led to the hot words.

They were simply arguing about whether or not they should carry thermos bottles of tea to drink on the long, tough climb that lay ahead.

It was August 1953, and this was a distinguished group of Californian mountaineers: Al Baxter, philosophy professor; William Dunmire, graduate student of wild-life; Dick Houston, physical science teacher; William Siri, research biophysicist who went from the Himalayas to the South Pole; Allen Steck, ski-hut manager; and William Long, United States Air Force survival instructor.

The early-morning argument petered out, and they took off their packsacks and started the stove. Fifteen minutes later the tea was made, and in harmony the climb began.

The route led from a small glacier on the south face to a higher one. Between the two were cliffs several hundred feet high. On top of the cliffs, the vertical wall of a glacier poised menacingly. At the bottom of the cliff, in the glacier they had to cross, was a deep avalanche trough, dug by the falling of countless tons of rotten ice. For two hundred yards they would be exposed to the threat that more ice would fall.

Now they were approaching the danger spot — and suddenly they stopped, frozen with shock. With a quiet swish the entire width of the lower glacier vanished beneath a cloud of snow and ice cascading from the cliffs above. But for the argument about the tea, they would by now have been committed to the crossing. Fewer friends from California might have gone on to the Himalayas.

These men reached the summit after sprinting, unroped, over the two hundred yards of no-man's-land. Long wrote of their success: "Pride filled us that we had reached the summit of such a fine mountain.

"Yet to a man we felt that if we were ever to climb the peak again, we would search out a route that might be more difficult, but not so exposed to the uncontrollable, devastating strength of Mount Robson, highest of the Canadian Rockies."

The year of their climb was the first season in fourteen years that men had been able to reach the peak of Robson. A few days earlier, David Wessel of the Seattle Mountaineers also reached the top. He wrote: "Climbers on Mt. Robson soon became casual about exposure from overhanging ice, for they travel almost constantly under the threat of avalanches or toppling seracs [ice-towers] on the final 4,000 feet.

"Thus far on our climb falling ice and big avalanches had occurred only at night. But when we passed under the lower glacier snout, a little serac crashed close to the last man. When the blurred images cleared, the last man was in the lead!"

There is, of course, a moral to all this: difficulty and danger, which seem to the non-climber to mean the same thing, are really poles apart to the mountaineer. The real mountaineer loves difficulty. This is the way he "travels hopefully" to arrive at his summit. Climbing the mountain is so much more worth while than sitting damp-seated on the summit, looking down at a view in which the soaring lines of the mountains fall far short of the sublime heights to which, from the valley look-out, they seem to aspire.

The more difficult the climb (within the limits of the party), the more enjoyable it is. It polishes the skill and technique; it stretches the limits of accomplishment, and makes the climber constantly devise new ways of overcoming complicated problems.

But the man who loves the difficulty generally loathes the danger, because few mountaineers – and none of the older ones – are the daredevil fools that the popular fancy would have them. There must always be a small amount of danger attached to any really difficult climbing – the possibility of misjudging a move, losing balance, or stupidly tripping over a rock. These are subjective dangers, which the climber can keep under control. They do not matter too much.

Far different – and infinitely worse – is the objective danger. This includes the possibility that an avalanche will sweep down on the climber; that a section of overhanging glacier will crumple and fall; that rocks, freed by the sun from their jewel settings of ice, will zip down with the speed of a rifle-shot, ready to brain the unwary.

On any big mountain these things happen constantly, because, far from being "the everlasting hills", our mountain ranges are in a state of constant disintegration, victims of an ever-losing battle with erosion. So one of the many facets of the mountaineer's art is knowing how to avoid these objective dangers and choose a safe route.

On some mountains, however, it is impossible to avoid them all. These mountains will always be dangerous to climb, and the man who would scale them must be prepared to take a calculated risk.

A prime example of such a peak is Mount Robson, which at 12,972 feet is the highest summit in the Canadian Rockies.

It is by far the best known of Canada's many major summits, for the Canadian National Railways route through the Rockies winds past its foot. Eighteen miles from its summit is Mount Robson Station, 3,150 feet above sea-level. Over the years many thousands of passengers have got out of the transcontinental trains on the brief stop-over there and marvelled at the huge dome of ice and rock looming almost 10,000 feet above them.

94

If they have come from the coast, the passengers have already been marvelling at the different type of scenery here. The peaks at the coast are often classical in outline, with pointed tops and precipices of granite that look almost seamless for thousands of feet.

The Rockies are a young range of mountains – a mere sixty million years old, compared with the 340 million years of some of the older stubs of ranges in eastern Canada. And their proud and turreted tops were once at the bottom of the sea. These are sedimentary mountains, made, geologists believe, from sediments laid down after the Coast Range heaved its granite spears up through the ocean and made of the land to the east an inland sea.

No fiery eruption of the earth shaped these mountains. But the pressures put on their strata by Pacific upheavals caused folding and faulting and cracking. Big blocks were lifted and slid over neighbouring blocks in a monumental face-wrinkling of the earth that moved the site of Calgary twenty-five miles nearer that of Golden, British Columbia. Then the irresistible tools of nature began to work.

The rain and the snow turn into streams that carry a sort of sandpaper suspended in their soft flow. The levers of frost and ice split rocks asunder. Cliffs of quartzite or solid limestone stand this better than the softer sediments, and so the familiar pattern of the Rockies evolved: bands of vertical cliffs separated by long slopes of scree, the slithering rock residue of slow destruction.

The once-flat beds of sediments turn into towers, castles, cathedrals – all with walls that look unscalable. But if on one side of the peak the weather-worn faults form down-sloping ledges, the up-turned angles on the other may make steps like a giant's causeway.

The monarch of all these masterpieces is undoubtedly Mount Robson. Long before Englishmen began their attempts to climb Mount Everest, some of their famous climbers came here to try Mount Robson – and failed.

The Robson for whom the peak is named is still unknown and probably always will be. Many people claim the honour for their ancestors, but none of the claims is very strong.

In 1862 a guide took gold-seekers past the foot of it. Of twenty-nine trips he had made over this route, this was the only time he had seen the top. He said the name was Snowcap or Cloud Cap Mountain. Less than a year later, Viscount Milton and Dr. W. B. Cheadle chattered their exploratory way by the mountain and noted that "a giant among giants, immeasurably supreme, rose Robson's Peak". They estimated it was between 10,000 and 15,000 feet high. It seems unlikely, from their journals, that they named it. If they did, historians suggest, it might have been in honour of the English actor Thomas Frederick Robson, then famous on the London stage.

Others say it was named for newspaper editor John Robson of New Westminster, British Columbia, who later became premier of the province. And in 1912, A. O. Wheeler, director of the Alpine Club of Canada, heard another suggestion. A Hudson's Bay factor, H. J. Moberly, told him that just before 1821, the Northwest Company of traders sent two hundred men into the Rockies under Peter Skene Ogden. These men, Iroquois Indians and French Canadians, scattered throughout the area, and, according to the story, the rallying-point for the return trip east was a camp in the shadow of the mountain.

The foreman in charge of the rallying-camp was named Robson. This sounds good, and as a story I would be prepared to settle for it. But once again the indefatigable historians, never content to let a good story lie in peace, demolished it with a bombardment of facts. They found a diary for 1823 in which a trading factor noted that everybody had so far failed to get into the area because it was so rugged – and this specifically included Chief Factor Peter S. Ogden.

An elderly Indian told T. C. Young of Jasper in 1913 that the peak was named for a white blacksmith named Robson who died after being kicked by a horse at Tête Jaune Cache, the junction of the Grand and Fraser rivers.

Another diary, kept by George McDougall, one of the first traders to cross the Yellowhead Pass, recorded of the Yellowhead Cache: "It is near the meeting of the Grand River – which flows from the base of Mt. Robson – and Fraser River." This entry was on April 25, 1827, but the original was unfortunately lost.

None of the earlier travellers agree on the origin of the name of the mountain, but they all agree on one thing – it was an inordinately difficult spot to get to. In 1907, when the first major attempt was made to climb the mountain, the party took well over a month just to reach it. On this party was the Reverend George B. Kinney, who became the most magnificent failure in Canadian mountaineering history.

Because of the lack of time, and bad weather, they were able to achieve nothing that year. In 1908 they met again in Edmonton: Mr. Kinney, Professor A. P. Coleman of the University of Toronto, his brother, and packer John Yates. Again it took them a month to reach the foot of the peak, a trip that today takes mere hours.

Then for three storm-ridden weeks they laid siege to the peak from the foot of Robson Glacier, on the north-east side, which is out of sight from the railway. Finally, when their time had almost run out, Kinney, angry and disappointed at failing twice in a row, set off alone for the sheer cliffs of the north face. He spent a shivering night wrapped in blankets, high above the tree line.

Then he wrote: "By the first light of dawn I was storming the heights. For thousands of feet, the great rock towered overhead, fringed and fretted with dripping icicles that hung in masses from the overhanging cliffs, sometimes as much as 50 feet in length. Narrow slopes of shale, at the foot of each wall, were as difficult to traverse as the cliffs themselves, for I had to plough knee-deep through freshly-fallen snow.

"I followed narrow snow-covered ledges that dwindled sometimes to but a few inches in width, while ever overhead hung those threatening lance-like icicles dripping their cold water upon me, for the warm sunshine now added these to other dangers.

"Ever and anon, with a report like a rifle, a chunk would break off from above and stab viciously into the narrow ledge near me, or vanish with a swift swish of flight into the silence of the gulf below. The steep narrow chimneys in some places were so full of snow that I would wallow nearly shoulder-deep before getting a solid foothold, and at other times I frequently had to shovel a way through over-hanging snow . . . .

"By 10.30 a.m., the last of those cliffs that had been deemed impossible had been climbed, and I stood on the summit of the great north shoulder at nearly 10,000 feet altitude."

He managed to get only five hundred feet higher. As he tried to get around to the west side, he suddenly ran into the most severe storm he had met in his life. It blew him off his feet three times, he said. Rather pleased that he had promised his companions not to stay out another night, he headed down.

Just as he came out of the clouds, he had a striking display of Robson's wanton power. "I was startled by a fearful explosion, then the whole face of the glacier crumpled up, plunged over the cliffs and swept into the valley. It took 10 minutes by my watch before the ice-boulders at the front came to rest in the bottom."

Mr. Kinney had seen many avalanches, including some that had tied up railway traffic for a week, but the "hurtling masses of that mountain of falling ice were simply appalling and far beyond all my previous experience", he said.

The next day was fine, and though they had decided to set off for home the whole party agreed to make one more bid for the summit, and then go home by forced marches.

They had an even closer view of glacier disintegration than Kinney had seen the day before. At one place, Kinney said, their old tracks vanished "under a million tons of ice". Another ice-cliff fell, and missed them all by only fifty feet. They kept on climbing, and according to their altimeters reached a level of more than 11,700 feet.

More difficulties beset them here, and they gave up their attempt – with Kinney deciding to try no more.

Mr. Kinney was an exceptionally strong man, both physically and in his determination. But that fall, when he got back to Victoria, British Columbia, he was disgusted with himself and resolved to leave Mount Robson alone in the future. As the winter wore on, however, his stubborn streak began to bother him. By the end of the year he had made up his mind that there was nothing he could do about it: he just had to go back and try again. He wrote to Yates, arranging to start several weeks earlier than he had before.

Robson had become more or less an obsession with him – and then in May he had word that some "foreigners" were planning to tackle the peak that summer.

It was a party of "foreigners" that would frighten any man who had come to regard a big unclimbed mountain as his own, for it was composed of some of the most outstanding British mountaineers of the day. They were Arnold L. Mumm, Geoffrey Hastings, and L. S. Amery.

Mumm had proposed two years before, on the fiftieth anniversary of the Alpine Club in London, that reconnaissances should be made of Mount Everest. That same year, 1907, he went to the Himalayas himself with Dr. T. G. Longstaff and General Charles Bruce. Bruce became the leader of the first Everest expedition, and Longstaff, on the 1907 expedition, climbed Trisul (23,406 feet), which remained for over thirty years the highest summit climbed anywhere in the world.

Hastings had been in the Himalayas in 1895 with two of the best-known British climbers of all time – A. F. Mummery and Dr. Norman Collie. Mummery vanished with two porters when he was trying to find a way up Nanga Parbat (26,621 feet) on that expedition. Amery, the third man, was a distinguished British statesman with a fine Alpine record.

These were the "foreigners" of whom Kinney heard, and they stampeded him into action. He sent a hasty telegram to Yates saying he was on his way, and on June 2 he set off. When he got to Edmonton a letter was waiting for him from Yates. This experienced packer, an expert on travel in the bush, warned him that it was sheer foolishness to start for the mountain so early in the season. Spring had been very late, and the peaks and passes were packed with snow, the letter said.

Kinney had no climbing companion, no equipment, and practically no money. Later he wrote: "But I had gone too far to back out then and snow or no snow I would make the attempt.

"On Friday, June 11, with only $2.85 in my pocket, but with three good horses packed with three months' provisions, I started off alone for Mt. Robson, hoping to pick up someone on the trail who would share fortune with me.

"For hundreds of miles across the prairies and through mountain vastnesses I fought alone the fearful difficulties of that trip, threading my way across treacherous bog or swimming my horses across mountain torrents.

"On the McLeod River I picked up an old timer who wanted to go along with me. Selling him one of my horses and half of my provisions, we shared together, for a few days, the joys and hardships of the trail. But the dangers of the trip and the floods of the Athabasca River were too much for him, so he dropped out and I was alone again, with only two horses.

"I nearly lost my whole outfit in the swollen Rocky River and my saddle horse and I had to swim for our lives. Then a mighty cloudburst flooded the entire valley of the Athabasca, beyond anything ever known in those parts before, leaving me stranded on a little island and

99

my horses on another, in the midst of those swollen waters. On that occasion I had to shift camp three times, wading waist-deep through the raging waters, carrying my provisions on my back to a place of safety."

A few days later he met Donald (Curlie) Phillips, an Ontario guide who was spending the season prospecting. Phillips had just passed six rather hair-raising days trapped on a small sand-dune island by the flooding Athabasca River. He was low on provisions, and was planning to head out for some more when he met Kinney.

In very short order, the minister had persuaded Phillips to join him on the climb. Phillips was twenty-five, and looked as strong as one of his own horses, but he had never climbed a mountain in his life, hadn't the vaguest idea of the techniques of climbing, and possessed no climbing equipment.

The spot where they finally made base camp on July 24 might have daunted any climber, but apparently Phillips' ignorance kept him from appreciating the real dangers. The Reverend Mr. Kinney wrote: "From where we camped, Mt. Robson rose in one sheer, unbroken wall from base to highest summit, and at such a fearful angle that a snow cornice, breaking from the crest, would fall 7,000 feet before it could come to a stop."

This was the same north side of Robson up which Kinney had stormed alone the year before. He was sure, from photographs he had taken from another peak, that by climbing the north ridge, and then crossing a big shale slope on the north-west side, he could reach the top by the west ridge. On July 26 they climbed the cliffs and set up "Camp High Up" at 9,500 feet on the shale slope. Once there, they changed their plan of attack, and decided that instead of walking a mile along the tedious shale slope they would tackle the cliffs directly above it.

They had a cold, clear night, and the weather, when they set off at the first pink of dawn, was perfect. But the cliffs were much harder than they looked, and the pair reached only 11,000 feet.

"The weather was glorious," Mr. Kinney wrote, "and the scenery of this show spot of the alpine world beggars description." Then he added, almost inconsequentially, "The warm sun kept the avalanches busy all about us and loose rocks would frequently whistle past. Sometimes these came from cliffs so high above that, without any warning and coming seemingly right out of the sky, they would scream past in awful flight to be engulfed in the silence below. We could hear them strike nothing either coming or going."

They went down for more supplies, and on July 28 pitched camp just above the shale slope, at 10,000 feet. Next day they tried again, and by 9.30 a.m. had reached 11,300 feet. Then their confidence was sharply jolted. Ahead was a cliff that even Kinney, with his muscles and his optimistic eye, decided was quite unclimbable. To one side, however, was a slope of ice at about seventy degrees that led to a spot twenty-five feet below the top of the cliff.

For more than two and a half hours Kinney hacked out a staircase of steps up this slope, and sweated up the difficult rock crack above it.

Now they were within striking distance of the summit, they felt. But as they moved along, the sun, swinging around to the west, began melting the snow that lay everywhere at this altitude. Ice began to crack and loosen rocks in fissures in the cliffs, and soon masses of rock and ice began falling all around them. They were above 12,000 feet by their estimate, but it was obvious that they could not reach the top and get back in safety.

Even to Kinney, with all his experience, the descent was a harrowing one. He wrote: "For more than a thousand feet down those upper cliffs of rock our every step was fraught with fearful danger. Not only did we have to get down gullies dripping and streaming with water, where falling rocks and avalanches were a constant menace, but the now-melting snow masses that covered every ledge threatened to slide from under our weight and drag us over the cliffs. We found the steps we had cut in the ice slope of the couloir below had nearly melted away, and that the whole mass looked as if it would slip down over the cliff if we so much as touched it. But it was our only way down, and we had to hurry, for each moment but added to our danger."

In the middle of all this, Kinney took time out to note that Phillips, who was using a stick instead of an ice-axe, "was fast becoming an expert in climbing". This must be a classical example of survival of the fittest! Either he became a good climber in a hurry, sharpening his natural aptitudes, or his career as a mountaineer would come to a sudden end.

The weather now turned sour, and storms kept them from the slopes until August 9. That day, beginning to feel familiarity with the cliffs, if not contempt for them, they began taking their heavy packs up places where they had had trouble earlier, even travelling light. They were at 10,500 feet when another storm began. They decided to keep going, up a sheltered, narrow gully.

Within a short time, three or four inches of snow had fallen, and suddenly avalanches began to swish by them. They tried their best to ignore them — even when one swept off Kinney's hat and whisked it out of sight below. However, somebody up there liked him. A few yards away he found a hat that had been blown off on an earlier trip here.

The slides began to get bigger, and suddenly they realized what a dangerous spot they were in. They put their packs under a rock and ran for it.

For three more days it stormed. The food was almost gone down at base camp, and they regularly ate stews of grouse and whistling marmots, a mountain ground-hog the size of a Persian tom-cat. They tried shooting mountain goats, but the rifle sight was so badly damaged that they shot off all their ammunition in vain. Five minutes after the last bullet was fired, a fine big billy-goat ambled sedately to within a few yards of them, and wagged his whiskers with a suggestion of a snicker.

It cleared on August 12, and quickly they packed up to the 10,500-foot level, and then worked their way along to a camp on top of the west shoulder. They dug down through two feet of snow, and lined their beds with dry, slaty stones before shivering through a bitter night.

The fact that the next morning was Friday the thirteenth did not bother them. They welcomed the morning — any morning — so they could start to move and thaw out their stiff limbs.

The weather was fine as they set off, but already more clouds were gathering on near-by peaks. The snow was firm, and they made fast time. Then a storm was upon them, and the snow began to fall lightly. Kinney was almost going mad with frustration. Heavy snow now meant bad avalanches on the open snow-faces above, he felt. And this had to be the last day, because the shortage of supplies would not permit another attempt.

Suddenly he noticed the snow was stopping. Only the occasional flake came down, though they were surrounded by thick cloud.

So they decided to chance it, and started up the very steep slopes, making the most of snow so firm that they could "just stick our toes in and climb up hand over hand".

Kinney recorded of this section: "For hours we steadily climbed those dreadful slopes. So fearfully steep were they that we climbed for hundreds of feet where, standing erect in our footholds, the surface of the slopes was not more than a foot and a half from our faces, while the average angle must have been over 60 degrees.

"There were no places where we could rest. Every few minutes we would make footholds in the snow large enough to enable us to stand on our heels as well as our toes, or we would distribute our weight on toe and hand holds and rest by lying up against the wall of snow. On all that upper climb we did nearly the whole work on our toes and hands only.

"The clouds were a blessing in a way, for they shut out the view of the fearful depths below. A single slip any time during that day meant a slide to death. At times the storm was so thick we could see but a few yards and the sleet would cut our faces and nearly blind us. Our clothes and hair were one frozen mass of snow and ice."

By now, Kinney estimated, they were within five hundred feet of the top. All around them were ice-feathers, like gargoyles chiselled in crystal, caused by the constant winds, and cornices standing out so far from the top of the walls that they were visible from ten miles away. The snow, unconsolidated by melting and refreezing at this altitude, was powdery and useless for making steps.

But they floundered, said Kinney, "to the very summit of Mt. Robson".

He continued: "I was astonished to find myself looking into a gulf right before me. Telling Phillips to anchor himself well, for he was well below me, I struck the edge of the snow with the staff of my ice-axe and it cut in to my very feet, and through the little gap that I had made in the cornice, I was looking down a sheer wall of precipice that reached to the glacier at the foot of Berg Lake, thousands of feet below. I was on a needle peak that rose so abruptly that even cornices cannot build out very far on it.

"Baring my head I said: 'In the name of Almighty God, by whose strength I have climbed here, I capture this peak, Mt. Robson, for my own country, and for the Alpine Club of Canada.' Then just as Phillips and I congratulated each other, the sun came out for a minute or two and through the rifts in the clouds the valleys about us showed their fearful depths. The Fraser lay, a thread of silver, 11,000 feet below us."

In 1913, the prince of Canadian guides, Conrad Kain, quoted Phillips as follows: "We reached on our ascent (in mist and storm) an ice-dome 50 or 60 feet high, which we took for the peak. The danger was too great to ascend the dome."

Mr. Kinney insisted they had reached the top. At the time, the Alpine Club of Canada accepted his claim. A few years later, when he went to Europe during the war, Mr. Kinney lectured to the Alpine Club in London about his ascent, and was made a Fellow of the Royal Society.

At the time he wrote: "I doubt if ever a peak was fought for more desperately or captured under greater difficulties than was that of Mt. Robson."

It was almost fifty years later that Mr. Kinney finally conceded he was probably mistaken, and that he had been a few feet short of the summit.

On that frigid day in August 1909, it had taken them five hours to reach their highest point, and seven hours to get back down to their upper camp because the snow was in such dangerous condition. By the time they reached base camp, they had been going for twenty hours, and were so tired they could barely eat and rest. The trip out was a miserable one – food all gone and trails in terrible shape after the floods.

On the way, the met the English party, who congratulated them most heartily. Mumm said: "Surely no mountaineering success was ever more richly deserved, or won by a finer exhibition of courage, skill and indomitable perseverance."

Phillips, the Ontario bushman who had just climbed his first mountain, noted after the meeting: "They seemed quite confident of being able to reach the summit of the peak, and said they had records of 20,000 feet.

"But there are mountains *and* mountains, and Mt. Robson is about as nearly impossible as they make them."

It was now September, with shorter days and worsening weather, and the Englishmen were to find that for them, at this time, Curlie Phillips had summed up the situation correctly.

So far the peak had been tried from the south, the east, the north, and the west. Now the Englishmen chose the north-east ridge, reaching it from the east side. Wrote Mumm: "A superb view it was, and we incontinently resolved to make an attempt on that side of the mountain without delay, being urged thereto by the weightiest of all possible reasons, namely, that Mr. Kinney had been up the other one."

With this party was Moritz Inderbinen of Zermatt, one of Switzerland's best-known guides, and one who had climbed all over the world. He looked at the mountain, and casually estimated that they would make it in about nine hours.

At 1.15 a.m. on September 7 the four of them set off. The weather was fine but much too warm, and soft snow delayed them considerably. By 10.30 a.m. they were on top of an ice-dome on the east side of the peak. Then on they went up the east wall.

Inderbinen, in the best tradition of guides, was doing all the hard work of chopping steps, and Mumm idly watched him work. He wrote: "I was tremendously impressed by the continued steepness of the climb. The slope on which we were standing was perhaps the steepest, and in Inderbinen's opinion it was the nastiest, bit that we had yet encountered, and the rocky belt above appeared literally to overhang, like the eaves of a roof.

"However, it was not very far off, and a little to our left a narrow neck in the line of rocks seemed to promise access to the final snow slope."

Then the sun went in, and a chill wind blew down from above, making Mumm feel a little miserable. His brain began to click and to work out details of the timing of the climb. At once he decided it was alarmingly obvious that if they went any higher, there was not the faintest chance of getting off the mountain that night.

So he flatly refused to go any farther. He was quite able to climb for another six hours, he said, but he would not spend the night out. Hastings backed him up; so they turned rather gloomily around, after a last look at the route through the rocky band of "eaves" above them.

Mumm wrote later: "We had scarcely started when a tremendous bang and crash made everyone stop and look around hastily over his right shoulder.

"A number of blocks of ice, some of them the size of a man's head, were just shooting through the narrow neck in the rock belt which had been selected as the best line of ascent, and an instant later came hurtling down the snow into the gully.

"Before anyone had moved or spoken another crash above heralded a second discharge. This one consisted of a mixture of ice and rocks and followed the same course as the other. They passed within a few feet of us, but nothing came our way.

"Very little was said, indeed there was little to say. 'We should all have been kilt,' Inderbinen observed thoughtfully a few minutes later (he meant if we had gone on in the direction originally intended) and that practically exhausted the subject." Later Inderbinen told Kain: "I never before saw death so near."

This was almost the last party to brave the terrors of the long bush trip to Robson. The Grand Trunk Pacific Railway was slowly pushing west through the Yellowhead Pass, and in 1911 the Alpine Club of Canada sent a three-month expedition to map and explore the whole area thoroughly, and to find a spot for an annual camp. The government contributed to the cost, and so did the railway, which wanted to know the best place to build a resort hotel.

Director A. O. Wheeler led this party, which included Conrad Kain, Mr. Kinney and Curlie Phillips, and photographer Byron Harmon. Wheeler was a surveyor, and his work on this trip reduced the official height of Robson from 13,700 feet to 13,068.

In addition to its ordinary camp, the Alpine Club held a special camp in 1913 as a result of the survey. It was based at Mount Robson Station and Berg Lake, and was confined to active members only.

In the years since 1909, George Kinney had been an important figure in the club. He was one of its formal "advisers" and his name was widely known among mountaineers. But it had gradually been accepted by many members that he hadn't *quite* reached the very summit. To the climber, the final few feet assume an exaggerated importance, as can be seen from the long battle for the main tower of Waddington, only sixty feet higher than the one the Mundays climbed.

It was felt among members that it was their duty to make the full ascent from this camp, and Director Wheeler, a dynamic man to whom present-day mountaineers owe a great debt, lost no time in picking a party to make the first attempt.

Two of them were Albert MacCarthy and William Foster, now thirty-eight and Deputy Minister of Public Works for British Columbia, who did such a tremendous feat twelve years later on Mount Logan. With them was Conrad Kain, a guide the club had brought out from Austria just four years before.

Their route was chosen for them in advance — the north-east ridge used by Mumm's party. Many of the arm-chair mountaineers who watched from the station assured MacCarthy and Foster that once they were on top of that ridge they could reach the south-south-east ridge, and that the peak was but a walk. Looking from the station, the south-south-east ridge is the long right-hand skyline. The route lay up the far side of that, then along the crest of the skyline.

The weather looked poor, but on July 30 they bivouacked at 7,000 feet on the Robson Glacier under the shadow of the Extinguisher — a name that would never have been bestowed in modern days, since the candle-extinguisher has almost disappeared. Like Kinney before them, they "feathered their nest" with rocks, laying flat stones in a mosaic at the bottom of a small depression in the ice of the glacier.

They were ready to move soon after 3 a.m., but on this northern side of the mountain it was not light enough to set out until 4.15 a.m. Even then it was dusk, and they stumbled as they tried to thread their way over ice-blocks and around crevasses. But by 7.30 they were on top of the Dome. Rising 2,000 feet above them was the sharp ridge they sought. It did not look too bad, but they were a long way from it yet.

They dropped a little to the start of the north-east face, and found a huge bergschrund gaping at the bottom of the cliffs. It took all Kain's skill to get over this; then he chopped 105 steps in the ice to get onto rocks behind it. Another blow: the rock that had looked to be full of good holds was in fact glazed with clear ice. Seen face-on from a distance, this wall looked vertical, icy, and absolutely impossible. In fact it was about sixty-five degrees. Now came another ice-slope up which Kain cut 110 steps.

Foster and MacCarthy, strong men themselves, were amazed at the strength of Kain. This was the place where Mumm had refused to go up the "overhanging eaves". Foster and MacCarthy watched the eaves apprehensively as Kain hacked on. Both offered to take spells at the tiring task of cutting steps, but Kain refused. "I must know my own steps if I am to come down this place," he told them stubbornly.

Soon after noon, they reached the top of the knife-edged ridge, ready for an "easy walk". So much for the arm-chair strategists and their theories thousands of feet below. Once again it had been shown that the only way to find out if a mountain can be climbed is to go and rub your nose against it: this ridge was no highway. Its crest, too narrow to walk on, disappeared into masses of ice, green and glittering where storms had swept it clear and piled dome upon dome. Far away, like something almost on another planet, shone the spire of the summit, invisible from the valleys.

They carved out a small platform on which to have lunch. As they sat, the sun moved slowly around, and suddenly they realized they could not go back the way they had come. The sun was melting the steps up the 2,000-foot wall, and already slides were beginning to slither down it. Their route was good only in the early morning, before the sun reached it.

On they went, cutting steps along the ridges just beneath its crest, on the south-east side. On the other side were overhanging cornices with pendant, glittering icicles.

The final slopes were festooned with ice formations more fantastic than anything any of them had seen before. They reminded Kain of giant ostrich feathers. Some of these ice walls were sixty feet high, and, as they wandered around trying to find ways from one terrace to the next, they sank to their waists in powder snow.

Finally they ran into the steepest ice of all — a gully that looked positively terrifying. Kain began once again the endless labour of step-cutting. Now, however, he had a strong wind to contend with as well. And the wall was so steep that he had to cut handholds so that he could hold on with one hand while he cut more steps with the other. It was exhausting work, but he thought of the pair below him as he cut.

They were already wet and miserable; now they were being sprayed with chips of ice from his flying axe. The rope was frozen and stiff as a wire cable.

He wrote later: "As soon as I was convinced that I could make it, I called to my *Herren*: 'Just be patient, the bad place will soon be conquered and the peak is ours.' Mr. MacCarthy answered: 'We are all right here, we are only sorry for you, I don't understand how you can still keep on cutting steps.'"

A few feet above this they were on a straightforward snow-ridge, and Kain turned to the others: "Gentlemen, that's as far as I can take you."

For a moment, said Foster, it was difficult to believe they were at the top. Then the small cloud-cap rolled away and an endless array of mountains appeared at their feet. They shook hands and Kain solemnly added his Alpine greeting of "Bergheil".

Foster said of the view: "In all, the vision bounded only by the horizon must have included 8,000 to 9,000 square miles of wonderful alpine territory, and awed too by the realization that this was but a tithe of the country's vast scenic heritage, little was said during the 15 minutes we spent on the summit."

The fifteen minutes, said Kain, were ten of pure pleasure and five of teeth-chattering. Their clothes were frozen solid, it was 5.45 p.m., and it was obvious they were going to be benighted. The route they had followed up was out of the question now, and they decided to go down the south side. This promised the possibility of getting much lower before darkness finally forced them to huddle among the rocks. Kain's motto on bivouacs was simple: "A night out is never pleasant, but above 10,000 feet it is always a lottery."

At one stage they found the only way down was by an ice-chute. But over the top of it hung walls of ice that might break off at any moment and sweep them down to destruction. Kain told the others it was practicable but highly dangerous. MacCarthy promptly replied: "Conrad, if it is not too dangerous for you, cutting steps, then don't worry about us. We'll trust to you and fortune." It took them an hour to get down it. MacCarthy came down last, showing a sure-footedness that astonished the guide.

The sun went down in a fringe of fire while they were still on the glacier below the chute. They pushed on in the darkness and finally stopped on a rock ledge six feet wide at about 9,000 feet.

The ledge sloped down and out, and they piled a few rocks to build up the spot where their feet would be. At first they roped together to make sure nobody rolled off in the night. But, each time one moved, the others had to move too; so they took the rope off. Just to the west of them, giant avalanches began to thunder down onto the glacier.

Kain dreamed of his native Austria that frigid night. He was close to a forest with branches and kindling everywhere. In the dream he reproached himself for being amid all this wood, yet not lighting a fire, although his *Herren* were freezing.

Foster dreamed that a long parade of friends came past him during the night, all carrying blankets. They all came up and said how sorry they were to see him sleeping in such a cold spot – and all went on their way, blankets still over their arms.

MacCarthy had a similar dream. He kept asking his wife to put more blankets on the bed. Her reply: "Oh no, dear, you can't have any blankets. Sleeping without any is good training if we want to go to the North Pole."

When they awoke, they almost felt as if they had reached the North Pole. The faces of MacCarthy and Foster were so badly swollen from exposure to the freezing cold and wind that they could not open their eyes. Not surprisingly, this worried Kain. He did not fancy leading two blind men down a series of crumbling cliffs and across glaciers slotted with crevasses.

He began to put cold compresses on their faces, and soon their eyes were open enough to give them a fair idea of where they were putting their feet.

It seemed a never-ending descent, with the pattern drumming itself monotonously into their brains. A cliff, an overhang, a ledge of shale; a cliff, an overhang, a ledge of shale. For thousands of feet it went on. The start was the worst. The cliffs were so steep and rotten that it took them three hours to descend eight hundred feet. After that it was more monotonous than terrifying. They crossed a hanging glacier and worked onto the south-west ridge, which Kain thought was the easiest route up the peak.

As they moved along he watched the west ridge, examining the route up which Kinney and Phillips had clawed and scratched their way so close to the top. It was, he declared, quite the most dangerous way that could be chosen up the peak.

Generously, he wrote later: "They deserve more credit than we, though they did not reach the highest point, for in 1909 they had many more obstacles to overcome than we; for at that time the railway, which brought us almost to the foot of the mountain, was no less than 200 miles from their goal, and their way had to be made over rocks and brush, and we must not forget the dangerous river crossings.

"Mt. Robson is one of the most beautiful mountains in the Rockies, and certainly the most difficult one. In all my mountaineering in various countries, I have climbed only a few mountains that were hemmed in with more difficulties. Mt. Robson is one of the most dangerous expeditions I have made."

Since those days, Mount Robson has been scaled by many mountaineers, including Norman Odell of Everest and Terris Moore of Alaskan fame. It has defeated even more, Frank Smythe and Rex

Gibson among them, and killed one fine mountaineer who was attempting it alone. For Mount Robson, whose remoteness once attracted explorers from the other side of the world, and which is now a prime target for tourist cameras, is a splendid example of why people do not conquer mountains at will.

A Great
Climber Dies:
a Hiker Lives

Many people seem to find something like magic in the mere size of a mountain: the higher it is, the harder it must be to climb. That is rather like saying that the bigger the apple is, the better it must taste. Many of the bigger mountains throughout the world's climbing centres acquire an aura of majesty and remoteness out of all keeping with the simplicity of ascending them.

Conversely, much of the essence of climbing – the inner jubilation that comes from craftsmanship and the defeat of the petty self – comes on mountains that are small and unknown to the non-climber. The whole world paid tribute to the men who climbed Mount Everest, the highest mountain in the world. Nobody but the addict paid any attention to the first ascent of Mustagh Tower, a 22,000-foot Himalayan peak that was in many ways much more difficult than Everest.

Hillary himself, after climbing Everest with comparative ease, was defeated in his own New Zealand by a peak less than one-quarter the height of Everest.

So it was on a small and unknown peak that Canada's best-known mountaineer of recent years climbed four seasons in vain and finally died. The mountain is Mount Howson, a little over 9,000 feet, which is between the Bulkley and Skeena rivers in north-central British Columbia. Heavily glaciated and bold in outline, the peaks of the area had never been climbed or explored before Major Rex Gibson first went there in 1954.

Rex Gibson was, at the time of his death, president of the Alpine Club of Canada. He had probably the most outstanding amateur climbing record in Canadian history – and many of the first ascents he made have rarely been repeated. In the Rockies alone he made over two hundred ascents, many of them on difficult peaks that had never been climbed before. With Henry Hall and Sterling Hendricks he made the first ascent of Mount Tiedemann, 13,000-foot giant neighbour of Mount Waddington.

During the war he trained many hundreds of Canadian alpine troops and was one of the few Canadian mountaineers to become a legend in his own time. In 1943, during an ascent of Mount McKinley in Alaska to test army equipment, he crushed five vertebrae in a violent convulsion at 15,000 feet. Yet he managed to descend the mountain virtually unaided in four agonizing days. His injuries were so severe that the army retired him on a disability pension.

This was the calibre of the man who made climbing Mount Howson his project. In 1954, 1955, and 1956 he came to its foot with assorted companions and tried in vain to find a way up its exceptionally steep faces and ridges. Bad weather blocked him, and unusual snow and ice conditions made routes he tried temporarily impossible.

In 1957 he came back again, enthusiastic as ever, though by now he was within three months of his sixty-fifth birthday.

His companions made up a distinguished group, all well known to North American mountaineers. They were Dr. Alexander Fabergé, 45, of the University of Texas; Sterling Hendricks, 55, one of the world's top agronomists, and chief of chemical research at the United States experimental station at Beltsville, Maryland; Donald Hubbard, 57, research physicist with the United States Bureau of Standards; and Alvin Peterson, 52, experimental engineer with the United States Ordnance Laboratory in Washington.

They were all fresh and fit from several weeks' climbing at the Alpine Club Camp in the Rockies when they arrived at Terrace on

August 6, and flew in a float-plane to Burnie Lake. They had eleven days for climbing before the plane returned to pick them up — and it rained solidly for eight of them.

On August 16, in perfect weather, Gibson, Hubbard, Peterson, and Hendricks set out to try the north ridge and east face. But new snow piled up by the storm stopped them on the glacier, and they were worried by avalanches hurtling down the face.

With their climbing time almost up, only one potential route remained — the west ridge. The best they could say of it was that it looked steep but feasible. Fabergé and Peterson decided they were not particularly interested in attempting this route; so on Saturday afternoon the remaining three left camp in Sandpiper Valley, planning to set up another camp on top of the South Col, not far from the foot of the west ridge.

Thunderstorms forced them to camp at the foot of the slopes leading to the col, but at 6 a.m. on August 18 they set off. The day was perfect, and in an hour they were on top of the col; in another, they were at the foot of the west ridge. Soon they were climbing a small ridge a little to the south of the real west ridge. The rock-climbing was ideal as Hendricks led up easily, with Gibson at the other end of the 120-foot nylon rope.

It was a perfect day to be attempting an unclimbed mountain, and as they went along the broken, easy rocks Gibson pointed with his axe to the beautiful setting all around him. "When people ask me why I climb mountains," he said, in his rather gruff and autocratic manner, "I can't find words to tell them. But here is the answer: getting up here where nobody ever stood before, and looking down at a thousand square miles without a soul in it."

Hendricks kept angling right across the rocks, fearing that the rock rib would end in an uncrossable gap just out of sight. Soon he came to the edge of a deep snow-gully. It was about fifteen feet wide, with steep walls. Near the far wall was a chute about three feet wide, worn by the steady fall of rocks and ice from the cliffs above.

There were no particular problems here, Hendricks decided, though they would have to move quickly. The sun was starting to touch the rocks above, and it would not be too long before its thawing rays started the rumble of decay.

Just one hundred feet above their present spot, they would be able to see clearly if this route would "go" or not. The hundred feet was up the gully, and, as it was all on snow, they reversed positions on the rope. Few could equal Gibson on snow and ice, and throughout the years he had climbed with Hendricks it was their regular rule that Gibson would lead on it. He did so now, and set out kicking small steps in the hard-packed snow.

Hubbard followed close behind him, and Hendricks stayed on the rock to safeguard their advance. Rapidly the snow steepened and it was necessary to cut steps in it. When this is done by a skilled climber, it is a delight to watch. Rex Gibson was an expert with all kinds of axes, whether for chopping wood or for nicking a hair-raising route up an ice-slope. A single swing of the axe was enough now. Each time he swung, a spray of snow flew up, and there was a chink in the icy armour just the right size to take the edge of his boot.

He angled slowly up to the right, while Hendricks moved onto the snow and kicked larger steps. These would serve as a position where he could stand in balance, plunge in his axe, and pass the rope around it as a movable anchor for the others. The snow was so hard that he could push the axe in for only about half of its length, and he could not kick really big steps.

He looked up at Hubbard, then towards Gibson, who was only ten feet ahead of the second man.

To his horror, Gibson half turned in his steps, muttered a soft exclamation, stepped down in seemingly good balance, and then began to slide. He made no attempt to perform the climber's routine precaution in case of a fall on snow, which is to use the axe point as a brake. Climbers practise this over and over again to perfect it, so that it becomes an extra reflex; but Gibson made no attempt to stop himself. In a split second he bumped into Hubbard, just as his axe was poised for the stroke that would ram it into the snow for safety.

Hendricks felt sick with the knowledge that the biggest crisis of his long career was upon him. Hurriedly he scooped in the slack as the pair shot by him in a tangle of ropes and limbs. The rope burned his hands as he took the strain, but he held on.

Suddenly they were slowing down, with about twenty feet of rope still to run out. The falling men were in the avalanche chute now, Hubbard trying desperately to make the point of his axe bite into the icy surface. They had almost made it, and were hardly moving when they hit a drop of barely two or three feet.

It was enough. The drop came just as the slack in the rope was used up, and the strain came straight on Hendricks. He was instantly flicked out of his steps. The axe came out too, and in a moment all three were shooting down the gully in bounds of ten and twenty feet.

They bounced from wall to wall, sure that this was the end. Hubbard was telling himself off furiously for "missing the catch" when Gibson first fell. Hendricks was sure he was going to die. Each time he smashed into a wall, the pain was unbearable, and he knew that the next would be the last before he shot into the air and down the final cliffs to oblivion.

He consciously counted the shattering impacts – then at ten he heard a hazy voice shouting: "Don't move, don't move." It was Hubbard's voice, and suddenly Hendricks realized their plunge had stopped abruptly after two hundred feet. As the three of them, locked together in a cocoon of rope, dropped over a little rock wall, their combined momentum smashed through the snow cover at a point where a small stream had weakened the crust. As they rammed through the crust into a small hole underneath, the sliding stopped.

Hendricks had doubled up, covered in snow, and Gibson knelt unconscious with his knees in Hendrick's chest. Hubbard hurriedly freed Hendricks's legs and helped him onto a rock ledge five feet away. Then Gibson came around and shouted to have his arms released from the snow. Hubbard freed him and slid him over to the rock ledge.

It was a sanctuary, but a very doubtful one. It was ten feet long, four feet wide and sloped downwards at an angle of about ten degrees. So Hubbard quickly drove an iron piton into a crack above them and tied the whole party to it for safety.

Then for the first time they could examine their plight. It was grim enough. Gibson had a severe wound in his left temple. He was breathing heavily, only partly conscious, and seemed to be blinded. Hubbard had a broken leg, which was swelling fast. Hendricks had broken his left arm at the shoulder; several ribs were fractured; and he had a bad pain in his back, caused by several crushed vertebrae.

The discussion about who would go for help did not take long. It was more or less academic; badly hurt as Hendricks was, he was the only one who could walk. It would not be easy, but he knew better than most that the well trained body can take tremendous punishment. He had escorted Rex Gibson down Mount McKinley after the injury to Gibson's spine.

But Gibson then had two healthy men to safeguard him. How would Hendricks get down from here alone? They had two hundred feet of thin line with them, used for lowering themselves down cliffs. Hubbard offered to lower Hendricks down to the glacier below.

But they could not see all the way, and Hendricks did not know what he might run into that his injuries might make impossible. He decided to climb back up and retrace the route they had followed before the fall. Hubbard cut about seventy feet from the climbing-rope and passed him an axe and a few pitons, and he left just before noon.

Gibson realized he was going, and said, "Tell them to bring in a helicopter; that's our best chance for getting out." Then he confided to Hubbard, "He's a tough boy, Sterling Hendricks; he can make it if anyone can."

Hendricks did not really think he could, and set off with what he called "sodden thoughts" in his mind. He left his spare food and clothing with the two on the ledge, and headed slowly up.

Eventually he regained their line of ascent, followed it a little way, and prepared to rope down a fifteen-foot vertical drop. Normally this consists of hammering in a piton, passing the doubled rope through a ring in the end, and then lowering oneself with the rope wrapped around the body to provide friction. Experts can descend in perfect safety at what appears to be almost the speed of a free-falling body.

But with broken ribs and shoulder, Hendricks could not wrap the rope around his body. He experimented with many variations and finally found one that was not too agonizing. Still, it took him an hour to get down the fifteen feet. Then he tried another drop, but after he reached the bottom of it, the rope stuck in the ring thirty feet above when he tried to pull it down after him.

He could pull with only one arm, and he struggled in vain for a long time. At last he gripped the rope with his teeth as well, and managed to worry it free.

It took Hendricks six hours to get back to the foot of the ridge. Then he stumbled across the small glacier and prepared to descend from the South Col to Sandpiper Valley, where he knew Fabergé and Peterson would be waiting.

When darkness came he was still two hundred feet above a very steep glacier slope he had to cross to reach the floor of the valley. It froze that night, and he sat for hour after hour breathing between his clothes and his body to keep warm. As soon as the sun rose, he began to move again, but he found the snow so hard that he knew he could not check a slide once it began. He waited until 10 a.m., hoping the sun would soften the surface.

By now he was desperate. His friends on the ledge would have to spend a second night out, and that might be the end of at least Gibson. So he carefully wrapped the rope around and around his body in the hope that it would provide friction to stop him if he slipped, and set off down. He did slip – twice. To his astonishment, the friction did stop him, but after the second stop he was terrified to find that he could not get up from his flat position in the snow. The frightening thought that he might just die there helpless in the snow spurred him on, and by rolling and painful manoeuvres he was able to get up.

At 4 p.m., after twenty-eight hours, he reached the sheltered calm of base camp, and tried to tell Peterson what had happened. He was so incoherent that for a long time Peterson could not understand him. When he did, he ran the three miles to Burnie Lake, where Fabergé had gone to tell the pilot to come back later. Just as Peterson was gasping through the last few trees to the lakeside, the plane took off.

Back at camp, the pair of them treated Hendricks as best they could, put him into a sleeping-bag with food and water, and set out to help the others. That night they camped at the Col, and first thing the next day headed up the mountain, dreading what they might find.

On the ledge, Hubbard had been making some grimly realistic calculations. Gibson would not live past Tuesday night, he thought, and there was no chance of rescue coming before Tuesday at the earliest.

His had been a bitter experience right from the moment Hendricks had left them. A few minutes after he disappeared above their heads, Hubbard lost track of Hendricks, even unable to hear any sound of his progress down the mountain. He was constantly worried by his knowledge that this is remote and unforgiving country. A minor injury can become a major problem after a week of ill-treatment. In some of the wildest ranges in the world, there is often a trail of sorts near by, and natives are available to share the heavy work of rescue. In many parts of the Coast Range of British Columbia it would be at least a week before help could be brought.

Rex Gibson was conscious for much of Sunday after Hendricks left.

On Monday, when avalanches began to pour down the gully — one so close that it buried their feet, he began to get worse.

In the afternoon he began to imagine his own rescue. He showered alternate orders and praises on his rescuers as they tried to get him to the helicopter that had just landed on the glacier at the foot of the cliffs. On Tuesday he was sinking fast. He had one lucid moment when he said to Hubbard, with a half-grin, "Getting rescued was a wonderful dream."

Just before noon he died. Quietly, alone in the natural cathedral of a big mountain gully, Hubbard sang a hymn and spoke the words of a prayer.

Little more than an hour later, Hubbard heard the sound of a rock falling, apparently from above. His hope of rescue faded instantly. He was sure it had been dislodged by Hendricks, trapped above and unable to guide rescuers to the scene.

But the sound came from below, reflected by a trick of cliff acoustics. A few minutes later Fabergé and Peterson climbed into the gully beside him.

The struggle was still far from over. They strapped his broken leg, made a supporting staff of tent poles, and slowly took him down. It was Thursday before they reached the lake and were flown out to Terrace.

A party from the Mountain Rescue Group immediately prepared to rush to the scene, but indecision by the authorities delayed them. Finally Rex Gibson's own wishes dictated that his body be left on the mountain. Time and again, his wife said, he had insisted that if ever he should die in the mountains, nobody should risk a life to retrieve his body. It lies there still, a part of the mountains that meant so much to him.

Thanks to Rex Gibson, Mount Howson has now been climbed. In 1958 the Alpine Club of Canada sent a party to the area to erect a memorial cairn and climb the peak if possible.

Conditions were vastly different from those of the year before, and Bill Lash, John Owen, and Adolph Bitterlich reached the summit from the north.

On the South Col, facing the rising sun, they built a cairn to honour a man whose enthusiasm kept him young when other men feel that worth-while life has passed them by.

After they returned, Lash wrote: "This monument we hope will long stand in the country he loved, even as his spirit will endure in the lives of his many friends and fellow members of the Alpine Club."

These men had years of experience facing the dangers of high mountains. They knew that accidents can happen, just as men have been killed playing football or crossing roads. That Rex Gibson should die at such an easy place seemed incredible, but his companions knew that in every valid adventure there must always be an element of risk.

The worst mountaineering accident in Canada's history happened in 1955 to a group of boys who had no idea of the risks they were taking. Seven of them died quite needlessly.

On July 8, a party of twenty-two boys arrived at Banff in the Rockies on an exciting holiday. They were all sons of well-to-do families and were making an expedition sponsored by the Wilderness Club of Philadelphia, Pennsylvania. Leading them were two camp counsellors, Oliver D. Dickerson, a teacher at the University of Pennsylvania, and William H. Oeser, a public-school teacher in Baltimore, Maryland.

First they scrambled up Mount Rundle, an easy mountain that attracts many tourists each year. Then at 9.30 a.m. on Monday, July 11, seventeen of them set out to tackle Mount Temple, which is 11,636 feet high. Some wore sturdy boots, others were in spiked baseball boots or track shoes. Most were in light clothing.

Oeser did not like high altitudes, and when they reached 8,500 feet he dropped out, though he was the only adult with the group. He told the boys, whose ages ranged from twelve to sixteen, to carry on, "providing it was safe". He warned them to come down quickly at the first sign of danger. Then he sat on a rock to watch, to wait for them, and to admire the beautiful scenery.

He saw that some of the boys dropped out a little higher up, at 9,000 feet, and that eleven of them went on. The most experienced of the eleven was Tony Woodfield, 16, who had been climbing mountains since he was nine. Slowly they worked up, crossing a snow-field, until they were at 10,000 feet.

Oeser was watching them, and he told the inquest later: "After sitting and talking for a while, I noticed the party starting down. They were a long way off, just vertical lines in the snow to me, and I saw them come together and stop on a rock. Then I noticed them start down again, and noticed a peculiar sort of rolling.

"I thought they were fooling around, and when the rolling stopped I saw people walking around, and was not particularly alarmed."

High above him, young Woodfield had been alarmed for some time. "On the way up we had seen several small avalanches," he told the inquest. "We turned back because of that.

"I heard and saw the avalanche coming towards us. I yelled 'avalanche', dug my axe into the ice and held on." The length of manilla rope snapped just below him, and the rest of the boys were bowled down the mountain side.

As soon as the movement stopped, Tony Woodfield rushed down to help. "I heard William Watts crying under the snow, and used my shoe to dig him out. I got everything out but one leg." But William died before help arrived, seven hours later. Oeser heard calls for help and went up, but there was little he could do.

Dr. Geoffrey Sutton of Banff arrived at the scene just after midnight. He reported that James Baylis, 13, whose twin brother Richard was also killed, died at the instant the stretcher arrived. Other victims were William Wise, 15, Miles Marble, 12, David Chapin, 15, and Luther Seddon, 13.

Only Woodfield and Peter Smith, 13, of Paoli, Pennsylvania, escaped unhurt. The remaining two, Frederick Barrard, 13, of Philadelphia, and Jerry Clattenburg, 14, of Rye, New York, were injured.

Dickerson blamed the tragedy on lack of information from the National Parks office. When they visited the office, he said, they could not find anyone who knew anything about mountains. No wardens were available, so they mentioned to the girls in the office that they planned to climb Mount Temple.

The girls made no comment, he said, and gave no indication that there was an avalanche hazard on Mount Temple.

"We took every possible precaution before climbing the mountain," he claimed. "The only thing that could have possibly hurt us was what did."

The jury found that "all leadership and equipment . . . was inadequate for this type of climbing", and absolved the Parks Department of all blame.

Chief Warden Bertram Pittaway summed up the whole sad tragedy with these words: "One competent guide could have taken all the boys up, but by the rock approach, not the snow.

"The only place where there was snow was in a bowl on the mountain, and it was completely against mountaineering principles to cross it."

Most mountaineering accidents, by their very nature, happen in remote places, accentuating the difficulty of search and rescue operations.

But perhaps the most celebrated search in Canadian climbing records was on a mountain that fills the picture windows in the homes of many of Vancouver's half-million people.

For six days the feverish search went on. One man escaped by himself from the tangled bush and precipitous bluffs of Mount Seymour. Then the body of one of his companions was found. And finally, when hope had almost been abandoned for the third, he was found alive in a tiny eagle's-eyrie of a cave. His rescue was one of the most dramatic ever recorded in Canada.

A few miles away in the unfamiliar hinterland, and it would have aroused little interest. Here on a mountain barely outside the city boundaries, in view of half the population of British Columbia, most of the residents could identify themselves with a man whose chances of survival had been fading quickly before their eyes.

Mount Seymour is a small mountain by comparison with the giants that rise in the Coast Range just to the north. It is only 4,758 feet high, but it is one of the best-known mountains in the country. It is a provincial park, and a good highway climbs in gentle twists right to the 3,600-foot level. In summer its trails are freckled with hiking families. In winter, so many skiers furrow its snow-slopes that the road often has to be closed before noon on a sunny Sunday.

It has become familiar to untold thousands. And this familiarity, while not exactly breeding contempt, has made most of them forget that a 4,000-foot mountain can be quite as lethal as a 10,000-footer when conditions are bad.

Those exquisite veils of gentle mist, shimmering in the late afternoon sunshine and caressing the eye of the novice, can turn within minutes to a clammy, bewildering blanket of fog.

The mountain is a frighteningly different place then. At one moment the bright green of the trees and bush, the wide and distant horizon, are almost tangible. The spirit sings, the way is clear, and the only sadness in the universe is your pity for the poor masses in the city below your feet.

You hardly notice the cloud steal in, if you are not trained to watch.

Suddenly north, south, east, and west are all the same direction. The warm sun dies out, and you shiver slightly. The friendly trees turn stark and black; the wide and adequate track beneath your feet becomes a grey and muddy thread that splits three ways.

Which way? Where am I now? Why does nobody answer the shouts that hang muffled and sterile in the cotton-wool world of a cloud?

If you are foolishly alone, the sudden pain of panic may tie a small knot in your stomach. If there are three of you, nobody really admits he is lost. Nobody confesses that he is worried. But there are three small knots in three tight stomachs, hardly noticed because of the confidence each draws from the presence of the others.

That is the reason why there was no noticeable panic at first on Sunday, October 14, 1956. All the three men involved were Scots, who had done a lot of mountain hiking in their own country and had often taken a quick hike up Mount Seymour since they had come to live in Canada.

They were Gordon Macfarlane, 27, Robert Duncan, 23, and Alick Patterson, 24. They were not planning anything ambitious — just a quick trip along the Alpine Trail to take a little of the city's smog from their lungs. It was late in the afternoon when they left the car at the end of the road and hiked quickly up the trail. It was a miserable day, with all the signs of a storm coming on, and less light even than usual at that time of day in the middle of October.

They had not reached the first of the three separate summits of Mount Seymour before they were forced to turn back. As they headed down, the cloud caught them, and in a very few minutes they realized they were lost.

The section of trail just south of the first peak wanders along a comparatively flat ridge. It meanders in and out of little gorges and makes numerous turns and twists. At one spot it turns abruptly to the left and slightly uphill. To a hiker going downhill, the obvious line is straight ahead, down into a gentle rock-walled gully. So many people have been led astray here that a false section of "trail" has been worn through the heather. Wrapped in the fog, the three men went down it.

They hadn't the faintest idea where to go next, but as there was still an hour of daylight left they decided to get lower down the mountain. Already it was raining, and they feared that during the night the rain would turn to snow.

The slope they were on was the western flank of the mountain. It starts off gently; then from a bowl beneath Suicide Bluffs it plunges 2,500 feet down to the Seymour Valley. The entire mountain flank is an intimidating tangle of canyons and creeks, bush and fallen trees, and steep cliffs often covered with slippery green moss. It is the worst sort of terrain in the world for travelling, and vastly different from the open, rambling country of Scotland. No trails exist down the slopes because they are in a reservoir watershed, closed to the public.

By now, the three were sure of being benighted until the fog might lift next morning; so they looked for a cave among the damp and gloomy cliffs. They found one, and tried to make themselves comfortable.

Patterson and Macfarlane did not smoke and carried no matches. Duncan had a lighter, but try as he would he could not start a fire in the damp twigs and leaves — even when he tried with a five-dollar bill. There was no worry about stretching their food. There was none at all, not even a chocolate bar.

The cave turned out to be a poor shelter. Gusts of wind swept the rain in on them, and they slept only in snatches, punctuated by shivering. They were not really frightened, however — just annoyed at themselves for getting lost so easily. They felt sure that when the fog cleared on Monday morning it would be a simple matter to find their way back to the trail.

When daylight eventually came, the rain was pouring down and the cloud was thicker than ever. "We were not even sure then what side of the mountain we were on," said Duncan. "But we came down a little, in spite of the weather, looking for better shelter. We found a good place after about two hours of walking, and decided to rest again. It was really just an overhang but it kept out the rain, and we crouched inside until noon.

"By this time Macfarlane was getting anxious about his wife. He figured we should make a break for it, but Alick and I argued against it. The rain was pelting down, and I knew it was best to sit it out. I guess we discussed it for about ten minutes, lying there trying to keep warm.

"Suddenly Gordon jumped up and ran outside. He said something like 'I've got to get back to my wife.' He was pretty desperate. I shouted to him to come back, as it was more sensible to stay where we were until the rain let up. But I got no answer."

All through Monday and the cold wet night, the other two huddled together in their cave, trying to keep warm. And at daylight on Tuesday, the weather showed signs of breaking.

So did the strength of Alick Patterson. On Monday he had been feeling very hungry, and to ease the pains he drank time and again from the rivulets and creeks they passed. When he tried to move out of the cave Tuesday morning to work his way down to safety, he was sick. "By the time I had gone ten yards," he said later, "I knew I wasn't going to get far."

Duncan did not want to leave him, and they went back into the cave to discuss it. Patterson insisted that as he was too weak to travel Duncan must go and bring help. Far below in the Seymour Valley, at a big bend in the road, they could see police cars and groups of searchers. They looked tantalizingly near, yet cries for help withered and died unheard among the cliffs. Finally Duncan agreed to go, but before he went he built a wall of rocks at the outside edge of the cave to serve as a windbreak. Just beyond it the floor plunged about five hundred feet to the bed of a creek.

It was now late on Tuesday, and for the second day searchers were working their way along the upper slopes of the mountain, hoping to find a clue to the route taken by the three men. I was one of them, and I found it difficult to make up my mind about the seriousness of the situation. A party of three was much safer than one or two, as one could always go for help alone if there was a minor but awkward accident.

However, if nobody showed up by Wednesday, it might well be because some tragedy had engulfed all three. It was easy enough to imagine a dozen sets of circumstances that could lead to this.

On Wednesday, Robert Duncan emerged from the bush at the foot of the mountain, where the farthest sprawl of urbanization has eroded a small street into its forest. His feet were swollen, and he was exhausted, but at last the searchers were able to get a lead on where his companions were.

It was already too late to help one of them. An hour and a half after Duncan left the cave, he had seen Gordon Macfarlane's body on its side in the bed of a creek far below. Carefully Duncan climbed down the steep side of the gorge through which the cataract tumbled, and took his friend's hand to seek the pulse. "But I knew he was dead by then," said Duncan, "and had been for some time.

"I suppose you could say it was touch and go for me before I saw Gordon lying there, but the sight of him just drove me on, seemed to give me extra stamina."

He presumed, from the cuts on Macfarlane's face, that he had fallen down the steep bank and drowned when he fell senseless into the water. An autopsy later showed that Macfarlane didn't drown – he died of exposure. Dr. T. R. Harmon said that the bruises and cuts on his head were superficial and would have caused nothing more than momentary unconsciousness. He speculated that Macfarlane had stumbled into the creek in the dark, and had climbed out and fallen back in several times before finally collapsing of exhaustion partly in the creek.

The terrible journey out through the bush had confused Duncan, and though he tried to show the search-master, Bill Angus, where he had left Patterson he could do little more than indicate a general area.

On Thursday, we tried to follow Duncan's route back up the creek, looking for the body. First I set off with a party led by Jack Atkinson, a mountaineer and water-board official. Down in the valley that day the rain was so heavy that creeks burst from their banks and caused widespread damage. Up on the mountain it was almost indescribable and seemed as bad as it could possibly be.

Suddenly the dark grey smother of cloud that engulfed us turned almost navy-blue, and it began to rain as I had never seen it before. The feeble sound of the human voice vanished beneath an absolute avalanche of sound as thunder detonated in the eerie air above our heads. For long and frightening minutes we were deafened by the explosions at the centre of the storm – and even when the focus passed, the roaring creek and rainfall would have drowned out any cry for help.

Several of us left the main party shortly afterwards and traversed the slopes to the next creek north. Atkinson and his men found the body a few minutes later.

Now the search was narrowing, and Macfarlane, who had been unable to help his friend in life, was able to do it in death. The position of the body once more limited the area in which we had to search for Patterson. Now the search could be restricted to the small area that actually led down into the creek.

But what an area it was. A thousand men could have hidden there, in the tangled tentacles of alder and berry bushes, behind the countless rocks, or in the canyons where waterfalls foamed white after the storm.

Friday was no day for searching. Bad as Thursday's conditions had been at the lower levels, Friday's managed to surpass them. This time we were working down from a higher, colder elevation. A combination of rain and snow was falling heavily, and after a few hours our party was soaked and shivering, hands and feet numb and wrinkled from long soaking in water that only barely escaped being ice.

Most, sensibly, turned back and headed painfully upwards. Three of us stayed. With me were Eric Brooks and Dr. Vernon C. Brink, two of British Columbia's most experienced climbers, whose long records had convinced them that, bad as things seemed, they might have been worse. We continued down, in canyons where the roar of waterfalls was so thunderous that there was little chance of finding a man save by stumbling on him.

Hours later, we too realized that it was not our day for miracles, and headed up. Higher on the slopes, six inches of heavy wet snow had fallen since we went down, and it was hard going. By the time we reached the top, we were hardly able to move along the trail back to the lodge.

Brooks and Brink said feelingly that in all their long experience this was the most miserable and wretched day they had ever spent in the mountains — a feeling with which I heartily agreed.

The weather cleared the next day with the sudden whisking-away of clouds that is one of the unfailing delights of living in a maritime climate. Few really believed that Patterson would now be found alive, though we all knew it was quite possible. The will to live has performed far more astonishing feats than this.

On that Saturday morning, as the biggest search-party of the week went out, I stayed home for the first time. The main reason was that every stitch of mountain clothing I had was still sodden, and so was the motley collection I had borrowed from my neighbours.

Patterson was found alive. It was just about 1 p.m., and he saved his life by what the rescuers called "a horrible sound, a hysterical howl that made our hair stand on end".

It carried more than half a mile down the mountain side, against the noise of a waterfall, and still was distinct enough to upset the six who heard it.

The cave below Suicide Bluffs, according to Joe Hutton of the British Columbia Mountaineering Club, a member of the first rescue party, was an "eagle's eyrie, a place where it would have been utterly impossible to find a man unless he could shout and wave".

I knew what he meant when he told me later that he had found, less than a hundred feet above the cave, an imprint of the distinctive nailing of my climbing-boot. Brink, Brooks, and I had stood there on Friday shouting ourselves hoarse while Patterson huddled back against the dry wall of his shelter. He heard nothing. And Hutton said that on the Saturday, though he knew rescuers were working in Patterson's cave, he could hear nothing of them as he stood on the same spot.

It was at once the best spot and the worst spot on the mountain for Alick Patterson. It was perhaps the driest, with the cliff projecting many feet out over his head. And it was one of the hardest to find. Cyril Scott, another of the rescuers, said, "How they got into that spot I just don't know. Everything is steep, and the floor of the overhang drops off almost sheer for more than five hundred feet to the bed of the creek." That very fact almost turned the astonishing climax of the search into a new tragedy. By the time they spotted him, Patterson was almost unable to move. Only his will power could push him to make a frantic effort to attract his rescuers' attention.

Yet he came out and waved so violently, according to Bob Herbison, flying by in a helicopter called when first word of the shout was radioed, that it almost cost him his life.

"He was waving so frantically and wildly that I was afraid he was going to swing himself right over the cliff in his weak state," said Herbison.

By the time the helicopter could swing back for another look, six members of the British Columbia Mountaineering Club had reached

Patterson, and his immediate worries were over.

The party, led by Roy Mason, consisted of Hutton, Scott, Fred Smith, Russell Yard, and John Holmes. It was not entirely chance that made Holmes the first man into the cave. He knew what it was like to be lost and helpless. He was lost for eight days without food in 1953, in the mountains of Garibaldi Park, just to the north. He had even felt the way Patterson had felt two hours before, when he first spotted the far-away searchers on the other side of the valley and shouted in what Scott called "the most horrible tone I have ever heard".

Hutton said: "Cyril Scott and I heard it first. It was strong but indistinct. We were half a mile away, with a big creek between us. We were on the ridge north of the creek, and I thought the noise came from one of the Alpine Club of Canada party on the ridge to the south. Three minutes later we all heard it again and this time there was no doubt it was saying 'help, help, help'."

Fred Smith was sure it was a call for help – "but I couldn't believe anyone who had gone through what he did would have the lung power to yell the way he did. I thought it was a searcher who had come down from above and got into trouble."

They all headed for an open spot on their ridge and looked for movement. At last they found it – in the middle of a steep cliff at the 2,500-foot level. The terrain was so rough that it took them two hours to cover the half-mile that separated them from Patterson.

Lanky cabinet-maker Holmes, first to reach Patterson, said, "He didn't say very much. He made a vague sort of remark asking if we were climbers, and apologized for being such a nuisance and causing us bother."

Fred Smith swung down the twelve-foot wall into the cave seconds later and saw this picture: "He was all hunched up, with his head on his knees. He would lift his head for a second to talk, and his eyes would open wide, rolling up almost under his lids."

Patterson, a thin man at the best of times, was now positively gaunt. He had lost twenty-five pounds during the six long days without a bite of food. Scott, who had seen a picture of him before he went searching, remarked, "I certainly couldn't have recognized him as the same man."

But the rescued man, who comes from Hawick in Scotland, cheered up noticeably a few seconds later with the arrival of Joe Hutton.

Joe comes from Glasgow, not far from Hawick, and he had carried with him a small bottle of Scotland's most famous export. As he heard Hutton's ripe Scottish accent, Patterson asked with a grin: "What part of Ireland were you born in?"

In a few minutes they had made him comfortable. Extra socks were pulled over his own, spare clothing was piled on him, and he was placed in a sleeping-bag. They gave him hot sweet tea, and soup, and soon he was as comfortable as they could make him. But the comfort brought him pain. It speeded his circulation, and to feet whose blood-flow had almost died this meant agony.

He was grateful for the hot, life-giving drinks, though they were not what he really wanted, despite his six freezing days without food or fire. "He wanted", said Scott, with the air of a man who knows what he heard, but doesn't quite believe it, "a glass of ice-cold milk straight from the refrigerator.

"He told us that on Friday night he couldn't get to sleep because he was thinking of it. And he wondered what it would be like to drink a mixture of cold milk and beer."

All Patterson had to drink during his six days was some of the icy rain that deluged the mountain. To get even this he had achieved a feat that startled some of his rescuers. Said Hutton: "There was a stream about fifty feet away, but to get to it he had to climb in his shoes up a twelve-foot rock wall that our group of climbers used a rope on. He climbed it twice, then had to stop because his strength was fading. I don't know how he managed it at all in his condition."

After those two trips, Patterson could do nothing but crawl to the edge of his cave and spend long, laborious minutes catching a drop at a time as it dripped from the sloping roof.

But now all this was past, and the lonely little world of Alick Patterson was coming to life again up here in the middle of the cliff. The pattern for a spectacular rescue was evolving.

First, the Alpine Club party arrived. It included leader Ernest Smith, Elfrida Pigou, Ian Kay, J. J. Fairley, Denys Lloyd, Len Bavins, and William Howie. This group, too, had its quota of people who knew what it was like to be in trouble. Kay had fallen and broken his leg in a remote spot some years before; Bavins's wife had been evacuated by helicopter after being injured in a fall.

Then the RCAF's Vertol helicopter arrived, an improbable-looking machine with two rotors and nicknamed the "Flying Banana" for the shape of its fuselage. The pilot, Flying Officer Don Park, could not land the machine on the sloping mountain side, but radioed the rescuers to carry Patterson to a clearing higher up the mountain.

Quickly they strapped him into a stretcher and began the difficult, back-breaking job of hauling him out of the cave, over rocks, and through the bush to the clearing about two hundred feet higher.

"It was tricky," said Ernest Smith. "It was awfully hard to avoid touching his feet, and the slightest touch gave him a lot of pain."

Now it was almost dark, and the sweating, struggling men were tiring as they worked up the slope. Park flew in three more — David Main, Bob Herbison, and Ed Cosgrove. Hanging in space, he lowered them like spiders dangling from a gossamer thread of steel.

The minute the party reached the clearing and laid the stretcher on a log, the helicopter swept in, the most grotesque caricature of an angel of mercy that could be imagined. Wisps of cloud had followed it up the valley, shutting it out from the anxious knots of watchers above and below. It was so dark now that a powerful spotlight was switched on to illuminate the sweating scene below.

Said Smith: "The pilot did a terrific job. He held her steady as a rock about forty feet up, and at 5.25 p.m. they had winched Patterson aboard. To make things interesting, they had only one set of straps on the stretcher instead of two. So Patterson went up with his head lower than the rest of him."

Within a few minutes the giant helicopter had whisked him away to hospital. As he went, Dr. M. S. Wolochow, an Air Force medical man, spoke to him. "He told me he had thought he wouldn't make it alive," said the doctor. "He was amazed at the work and courage of the mountain rescue boys. He'd seen them on the road below during the week, and after the pounding they took on Friday he couldn't believe they were back looking for him."

Alick Patterson was safe at last, on the way to a recovery that was complete except for the loss of a few toe joints.

All that remained was for the rescuers to climb in the darkness over snow-covered rocks and bush to the main trail 1,300 feet higher. You would never have known, as they stumbled happily through the snow, filling the night air with wisecracks, that they had just helped bring a man back from the dead in one of Canada's most spectacular mountain rescues.

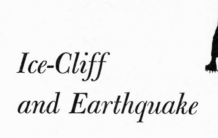

Ice-Cliff
and Earthquake

MOUNT FAIRWEATHER

Map on page x

Nine hundred miles north-west of Vancouver, on a shoreline thrashed
by the turbulent North Pacific Ocean, stands one of the tallest coastal
mountains in the world. It is a glittering peak, which for almost two
hundred years has been a guide to explorers gingerly probing the
mysteries of the wild, ice-chiselled coast of Alaska.

A map published after exploration of the coast in 1786 by the
French Captain La Pérouse shows the mountain as "Mont Beautems".
Today it is known as Mount Fairweather, and from its summit at
15,300 feet rivers of ice plunge right into the ocean.

Everest has a snow and ice zone of around 13,000 feet. Mount
Logan, the Yukon giant that rises to almost 20,000 feet, stands 14,000
feet above the general level of the terrain around it. Fairweather's
glacial armour soars more than 15,000 feet right out of the sea.

Dr. W. S. Ladd, an early Alaskan mountaineer who tried to climb it
in 1926 and 1931, was enthralled by its splendour. He wrote: "Its
pyramidal central summit, and broad shoulders approached only by
the steepest of great snow and ice arêtes, give delight in a symmetrical

grace and beauty that I know of [in] no other great massif. From an altitude of 3,000 feet, its fluted walls rise almost too steeply for the mountaineer on every side. The snow and the ice hang as if glued upon them. Upon every line of approach that the eye follows in an effort to plan a route to the summit, there is some obstacle demanding the best art of the mountaineer."

It would have taken the best art of the magician to persuade the early explorers to try to climb it, though several of La Pérouse's men set foot on one of the glaciers. For them, battling the gales and currents brewed in the hell's-kitchen of the wild Pacific weather, mere survival was enough. They were content to marvel — in the rare moments when nature would allow them. Calling this ocean the "Pacific" was one of the great misnomers of all time. Surely whoever first named Fairweather had his tongue in his cheek, going along with the irony of Balboa's blunder when he named the Pacific almost 3,000 miles to the south.

One tempest after another whines in from the vast, cold ocean throughout the winter. Bad weather is generated in low-pressure areas, and the pressure around Fairweather is so low, according to Allen Carpé, one of the earliest climbers in the region, that average pressures on its peak are about ten per cent lower than would be expected. They are as low as would be found on inland mountains of almost 17,000 feet.

The pressure may be low, but precipitation is high. For week after week, with rarely a break, snow falls steadily for most of the winter, piling up enormous drifts that make the landscape arctic. All along this brooding coast, the resulting glaciers rumble and fan out to the sea. The pocks and veins of age and decay now mar their once-white faces.

High on the slopes of the peaks the ice is still young and active, worrying and grinding at the age-old rock of the earth's hard crust. Here at the tattered fringe of ocean, many glaciers are stagnant. Steaming and sweating in the summer sun, they look like the worn-out limbs of a mountain monster that has outlived its day and withered on its suicidal rush to the sea.

Towering over the surrounding peaks, Fairweather was a striking challenge to the mountaineering pioneer. In 1926 Dr. Ladd made the first attempt to climb it. With him were two of the best climbers then active in North America — Andy Taylor and Allen Carpé, fresh from their great ascent of Mount Logan.

They reached a height of 9,000 feet, after an exciting time ferrying supplies ashore at Cape Fairweather through the rolling ocean surf. In 1930, Dr. Bradford Washburn took up the attack. He was to compile perhaps the greatest record in Alaskan climbing history, but that year he reached only 6,700 feet amid the jumbled pinnacles of ice. He did not have another chance, because Ladd, Taylor, and Carpé came back in 1931, with Dr. Terris Moore, later president of the University of Alaska.

Their expedition took two months, and the weather was so bad at the start that it took them ten days to make the trip by boat from Juneau to Lituya Bay that normally took twenty hours.

Moore and Carpé reached the summit after climbing through the night of June 7, and found that Dr. Ladd was right about the steepness of the snow-slopes. They measured great faces at an angle of fifty-five degrees throughout their length. In many places they steepened to sixty degrees. After it was all over, Carpé confessed to his friend Henry Hall that Fairweather was technically the toughest peak he had climbed in his outstanding Alaskan career. And when an account of the climb appeared in that year's *Alpine Journal* in London, the editor, E. L. Strutt, wrote in an introduction: "The ascent of Mt. Fairweather is, we understand, the hardest yet accomplished among the 'Arctic' mountains of North America."

Fairweather had fascinated me since just after I moved to Canada in 1952, but early efforts to attempt it shattered on the twin reefs of time and money. Then an oddity of geography and the centenary of British Columbia's birth suddenly made it feasible.

A glance at the map will show what I mean about the geography. Northern British Columbia's access to the sea is cut off for hundreds of miles by the Alaska Panhandle, a long strip of United States coastline. At the north end, the boundary of British Columbia reaches far out into the Panhandle. The boundary surveyors chose Fairweather as one of the boundary points, so that the British Columbia–Alaska border runs right over the top.

This made it far and away the highest point in British Columbia — and a peak so far unclimbed by Canadians. In 1957, L. J. Wallace, chairman of the committee preparing the centennial celebrations for

1958, thought it would be a good idea if a mountainous province could start the program with a mountaineering feat, much as the ascent of Everest opened the reign of Queen Elizabeth. On behalf of the Alpine Club of Canada, I suggested an ascent of Mount Fairweather, and this was immediately approved.

It is a fundamental principle of mountaineering that the difficulty and steepness of a mountain decrease in direct ratio to the distance of the challengers from the peak. Otherwise, of course, there would be few attempts on major mountains. Who, in his right mind, would cold-bloodedly plan to scale a difficult mountain if he could actually see the difficulties as he planned? When he actually sees the difficulties, of course, it is too late: he is committed!

In our minds we climbed Fairweather a dozen times the year before we even saw it. Optimistic routes were planned on aerial photographs, camp-sites were picked from the inaccurate map with a blithe disregard for the fact that the previous party had trouble finding even one place big enough for a tent. Ian Kay, our one-man technical planning committee, more or less "delivered" the mountain to us gift-wrapped, when he completed a masterpiece of planning on the assault schedule.

It came in the form of a series of tables, which would tell at a glance how long two, or three, or four, or eight men should take to reach the summit, how much food they would have to carry, and whether or not they should leave the tents standing on Day 3 when they left Camp Two. We were sure it covered every possible combination of circumstances on the mountain. But I was perversely glad to find that by a flagrant breach of organizational etiquette we finally attempted the summit by an "unplanned plan", in the best tradition of individualistic mountaineers.

There were several reasons why we suggested Mount Fairweather to the centennial planners. First, of course, it was time Canadians tried to reach the highest point of British Columbia. Second, it was a first-class climb, and regular progress bulletins by radio from base camp would, we thought, make a worth-while addition to the many other projects being reported, and focus attention on the least-known part of the province. Third, it would give the Alpine Club and the British Columbia Mountaineering Club experience in planning and making a major expedition which could help to raise the standards of both clubs in the years ahead.

Therefore, we set up many committees to look after various aspects of the expedition, and Roy Mason and I spent a hectic winter co-ordinating their work. The Royal Canadian Air Force came into the picture, and we earnestly discussed details of where our goods should be parachuted and how they should be packaged, and a hundred other details. Here again, nature knocked holes in our plans, and our elaborate, well-conceived system of alternative drop-sites had to be abandoned at the last minute.

The Canadian Broadcasting Corporation decided shortly before we left to send with us, at their own expense, a television producer and a cameraman. We had to start getting them into shape, so I undertook to hike with them, before work each day, up 2,300 feet of the steep ski-lift track on Grouse Mountain, a few miles from Vancouver. Michael Rothery and Kelly Duncan were the two who finally came, and they proved willing and firm friends of the whole party.

But the cameraman who showed up for the first early-morning training session was a bit of a problem. We had met briefly on several assignments, and he knew that I was a reporter. He had no idea that I was a climber too – in fact, by this time I had been named the leader of the expedition.

He was waiting when I arrived at the foot of the ski-lift, and said, "Oh, are you going too?" I confessed that I was thinking of doing so. Then he confided, "I don't know what all the fuss is about. They tell me this is just a promotion stunt. They say this mountain is so easy that our television cameras could be waiting on top when the party reaches there, and make a good movie. But the climbers don't want their glory stolen, and have insisted that we won't be able to go above 5,000 feet. They will take a camera on to the top."

I didn't ask him who "they" were, knowing that only one man still lived who had stood on Fairweather's top – Dr. Terris Moore, who was far away in the United States. So, very meanly, I murmured, "Well, that sounds interesting."

This encouraged him, having dug his own trap, to blunder head-long in. "This training program", he went on, "is just a waste of time. I used to be a national champion in cycling. I don't need any train-ing."

Up to this moment, I had been about to explain the situation to him as we stood around waiting for the late-comer. Instead I suggested we hike up without waiting for Michael. My confidant shot away up the slope at a great rate, and in the first hundred feet rapidly opened up a gap between us. I plodded along, and by the time we had climbed three hundred feet, I was a yard behind him, listening to his furious panting. Sweat poured from him, and I asked if he wanted to rest. He replied, "Okay, pant if you pant pant need pant the rest pant pant . . ." So while his heart gradually stopped its pounding, I told him the score and gave him a few pointers on how to make uphill travel a little easier.

He performed very well for a beginner, but on the way down he said he had had an ulcer some time before and was worried that he might have trouble if he were away for a month in remote Alaska.

When I reached home, I telephoned the expedition doctor, Denis Moore, and asked his opinion. "Well," said Denis, "tell him I think a month away from civilization will probably do his ulcer a world of good. If anything does go wrong, we'll be able to fix him up all right. It won't be quite the same as being in hospital, but we'll manage."

With visions of a flashing scalpel in a billowing tent on a glacier, I told him. Next day a different cameraman went into training.

Our climbing training had been under way for some months, with fourteen climbers getting into excellent condition for the final selection. I found some of the training was rather risky when we were not on the mountains. Each night through the winter I ran a couple of miles in the dark on the streets near my home. One night as I pounded down the road, a police car came roaring up and I was asked a barrage of questions. They had set a trap, it seemed, for a peeping Tom who was busy in the neighbourhood – and sprinting Sherman just answered the description nicely! Eventually I persuaded them I was crazy but harmless, and too tired anyway, so they let me go.

Another night, as I ran as hard as I could along the final stretch, another car pulled in beside me. The door was flung open and a voice shouted, "I don't know where you're going, Buster, but wherever it is I'll drive you, if you're in that much of a hurry."

We practised crevasse rescue techniques on the glaciers of Mount Baker, in Washington State, and completed the program by hauling fifty-pound packs to the top of the 10,800-foot mountain. We camped one night at the 9,000-foot level, and then set up our expedition tents for another night on the summit, giving our basic equipment a thorough work-out. This gave us, for a day, the delightful sensation of starting our climbing downhill, then making high-standard ice-climbs back up to the tent. Even the weather co-operated. For the climbing it was perfect. For the summit camp and the descent it turned into a howling blizzard that made route-finding difficult even with the green bamboo canes we had put up as markers the day before.

The eight climbers were chosen by a personnel committee headed by the veteran climber Eric Brooks. They were:

Paul Binkert, an astonishingly fit and able man of fifty who had amassed tremendous experience in Europe, the Andes, and Canada.

David Blair, born in British Columbia, with experience of many difficult climbs on British Columbia mountains.

Fips Broda, from Austria, an instructor in mountain warfare in the last war, with a fine record in the Alps, the Caucasus, and the Canadian Coast Range. I always considered him the climbing leader.

Joseph Hutton, a Scot, with wide experience in Europe and Canada.

Dr. Denis Moore, another recent arrival from Scotland, who had been climbing difficult mountains for years.

Walter Romanes, a quiet, incredibly strong New Zealander who had climbed in many parts of the world, and was at twenty-seven the youngest member of the party. A few weeks after the expedition finished, he was able, being a carefree bachelor, to dash back to New Zealand and join an expedition to the Antarctic. Later he went to the Himalayas with Hillary.

Russell Yard, a strong, heavily bearded climber who was the second Canadian-born member of the party, thoroughly at home in the tall, tough mountains of the province.

I came from England in 1952 after climbing in Britain and the Pyrenees, and was soon fascinated by Coast Range exploration.

Two more names were yet to be added to our roster. The centennial authorities wanted to issue reports on our progress, which raised a difficult problem. In the Himalayas, runners can often do the job. Here there were no trade paths or regular routes, just a wilderness of mountains and glaciers bordered by the ocean. A radio was the only answer — but we needed a powerful radio transmitter at the spot to be sure of sending our messages 1,000 miles to Vancouver.

The British Columbia Amateur Radio Association solved the problem by offering to put a complete station at Lituya Bay, twenty-four miles from our peak, and right at the base of operations. Two experienced "hams", George Kitson, a detective, and Ken McMillan, agreed to man the station for the whole month.

The climbing party carried a portable transmitter right into base camp, and the nightly chattering back and forth became essential listening for the many "hams" on the Alaska Panhandle network. They went to considerable trouble to make arrangements for us, and, once the climbing was on, obtained special weather forecasts for us every day.

The climbers kept their equipment down to a minimum and this was fortunate — for when the radio operators arrived at Vancouver Airport, they had a small mountain of sets and spares and generators. By the time it was all aboard and we took off at 8 a.m. on June 16, 1958, there was just no room for us to sit. We settled down among the crates, and flew until after 8 p.m. trying to get into Lituya Bay, which is about a hundred miles north and west of Juneau.

As we headed from Juneau towards the ocean coast, a solid wall of cloud built up ahead and forced us back. We tried again the following morning, despite thick cloud and rain. The pilots, Flight Lieutenants Don Hill and Ed Cameron, managed to creep down to within two hundred feet of the sea through a hole in the clouds, and we were astonished to spot a small aeroplane on the beach, only a few yards from the Pacific rollers.

Where it had stopped, a tent was set up — our first indication of the way Alaskan glacier and bush pilots seem willing and able to land almost anywhere. We also spotted Lituya Bay near by; so Don Hill offered to put the big Canso amphibian down on the beach near the other aircraft. The shade of green that spread over my face must have put him off, and instead we headed for the bay.

This had been gloomy and dispiriting work, with the crew doing wonders even to find the place, which is the only harbour for more than one hundred miles along this inhospitable coast.

Now, as we swung low over the surrounding trees, patches of cloud were hanging down almost to the water. Through the gloom we suddenly saw a dozen fishing-boats dotting the likeliest landing-place — and here and there the glint of icebergs from glaciers at the head of the bay.

This was the second try, and, like the first, it failed. Visibility was too poor to land in the circumstances, and gas was getting low; so back we went once more to Juneau. Morale was getting a little low, too, as we climbed slowly through the layers of cloud. Then, at 6,000 feet, we were on top of the weather for an instant. For perhaps ten seconds we had a view of Fairweather floating an impossible distance above us. A few obscure little brain cells did the rest, and in a moment everybody was enthusiastic once more.

Just before 3 p.m. we landed at Lituya and work got rapidly under way. Everything was most efficiently set up. The television boys were waiting for us on the beach, flown in earlier by bush pilot Ken Loken, to whom flying blindfold seemed to be second nature. A rubber boat was inflated, an outboard motor attached, and away went the first load. So did the motor. It swamped on landing and for the next couple of hours we rowed.

Only five minutes' walk from the sandy beach just inside the spit guarding the entrance to Lituya Bay was a small lake surrounded by tall timber. It was sheltered from the wind, had plenty of fresh water, and was ideal for stringing aerials for the radios.

It was raining when we left the radio camp the next morning, and we all carried big packs, but nobody cared. At last we were really on the way to our mountain. So far we had been passengers, but now everything depended on us.

The route took us a dozen miles along the ocean shore to Cape Fairweather, then a similar distance up Fairweather Glacier to a point right under the southern cliffs of the mountain. We expected the walk to be hard, trudging along twelve miles of shifting sand, but the day turned out to be one of delightful surprises.

First, we found a trail good enough for a park. It had been built by prospectors many years before, and we found many signs of their activity. A decayed cabin here, a broken sluice there where they had panned for gold, even the wreckage of an old steam-engine that had almost rusted away. The bears that abounded here had also made full use of the trail, and their big feet had worn deep, regular holes in the track.

In mid-afternoon we reached a camp of modern-style prospectors. Mark and Walter Gilkey, both in their sixties, had a very comfortable camp, every item of which had been flown in by the small plane we had seen the day before. They had found good showings of titanium, more precious than gold in this day of jet planes and satellites, and were enthusiastically planning to develop their claims.

Our walk from here made us feel ashamed when we reflected on our arm-chair visions of the tough travel in Alaska. We strolled through wonderful fields of lupins on a narrow fringe of land between the ocean and the forest. For literally miles we trod on beds of wild strawberries, with the occasional ripe one promising vitamin orgies on our way back from the peak.

Half an hour short of camp, the Canso roared at pebble-whipping height along the beach looking for us. The pilot radioed that he had dropped all our supplies – but at neither of the places we had selected in advance. The lower site was hidden in cloud, he said, and the upper one was an impossible maze of crevasses. So he picked the only reasonable place he could see, and dropped a marked map to guide us. Then a waggle of the wings and he was gone. We were on our own for a month.

That night we camped on the beach, sheltering under plastic sheets to keep out the spray from the sea. It was a most unlikely approach to a big mountain. As we turned in after 11 p.m., the sun was still shining brightly, the surf was pounding with a resonant roar, and porpoises leaped about in the waves. Just before we turned in, the little white plane sped by, and we waved. The pilot must have been dumbfounded to see us there with our roaring fire, and probably thought we were shipwrecked sailors. He banked and flew in low for a closer look. Finally we managed to convince him that we did not need rescuing just yet.

On June 19, we quickly reached a big river flowing from the foot of Fairweather Glacier, and there had our first ground-level view of the mountain. It was magnificent – and rather frightening. As Dr. Ladd had said, every side looked almost too steep for the mountaineer to climb. We lost sight of it almost immediately, ploughing our way through thick bush. In the three hours to lunch-time we covered only two miles.

On the way we first saw that peculiar Alaskan phenomenon, a stagnant glacier out of which a veritable jungle was growing. The ice,

here about a hundred feet thick, and right at sea-level, had accumu-
lated enough gravel and silt to support luxuriant stands of slide alder.
We were quite fascinated and intrigued — until we tried to make our
way through it. Alder, with its snaking, springy branches, is hard
enough to penetrate at the best of times. Now the footing was completely unreliable, as the slightest pressure from the boot sent the soil
sliding off the ice.

Soon, however, we had worked our sweating way through this and
were out on open moraine. This was easier going, but it, too, had its
problems, consisting as it did of millions of slabs of rock poised on the
dead ice. It was a huge moraine, dwarfing anything in Europe. We
threaded our way through vast piles of rock that looked like exaggerated slag heaps from Welsh mining villages. Some of the effects
were striking. On all sides were weird caves and grottoes with water
cascading in. Large chuckling streams of melt-water just vanished in
mid-gurgle.

As we went, we built rock-cairns, for we could see from the great
size of the moraine that we would have trouble finding our way back
across it in a fog. Camp this night was in a slate-lined hollow in the
ice half a mile from the active white ice of the glacier, about seven
miles from the air-drop. We were still sleeping out, as the tents were
in the air-drop, but we built small sheltering walls of rock, and made our
beds on flat rock slabs.

Within half an hour next day, we were on the main Fairweather
Glacier, ready at last to cope with something more interesting than
bushwhacking. It looked as if we would have plenty to cope with.
From here, the sweep of the glacier soared up in two vast steps to the
5,000-foot level where we hoped to put our main base camp. The first
ice-fall appeared easy enough, and we managed to pass it on the right
after several false starts.

Then, as we stood wearily, high on a side-hill late that evening, we
spotted the air-drop parachutes lying on the snow on the far side of
yet another glacier. They were in a flat and seemingly stable spot
right on our line of approach, and we blessed the good sense of the
airmen who had dropped them. We reached them at 9.45 p.m., after
almost 15 hours of travel.

The Royal Canadian Air Force had picked the only feasible spot in
the circumstances — at the edge of a small glacier coming in from the

south. All the thirteen parachutes were within an area of three hundred yards, a fine piece of precision dropping by Para-rescue expert Jake Dyck, considering the problems. Only one 'chute could be dropped at a time as the Canso lumbered by, and each time it had to circle a mountain, climb over a high pass, and then descend to the drop-zone. Again it would bank steeply and circle the mountain – all the time dodging layers of clouds.

It was the best site available, but, even at that, what a horrible spot it turned out to be. Within half an hour, six members of the party sank part-way into masked crevasses, which made recovering the parachuted parcels containing the tents a nerve-wracking business. We probed the snow until we found a safe area big enough to hold the tents, and marked it out with bamboo sticks. Nobody could leave this tiny camp-site alone or unroped. Five minutes after the last tent was up, rain began to fall – the first since we had left Lituya Bay three days before.

Here we were at 3,500 feet. The next day, Walter, Fips, and I set out to find a route beyond the second ice-fall to the 5,000-foot level, whence the steep south-south-east ridge sprang more than 10,000 vertical feet to the summit.

The ice-fall was a bewildering maze of decaying ice-towers, quite impossible to negotiate in safety. Time and again we saw blocks break off and collapse in a shower of splinters. Everything here was on a titanic scale, and it was hard to realize that often these pieces of tilted ice were bigger than apartment buildings.

On the south side of the glacier, however, we could make our way slowly along the mountain wall that hemmed the glacier in. This, too, was mostly glacier, steep and soft, but manageable. As we crossed one of the snow-bridges, the upper reaches of the mountain cleared enough to show us the final part of the route to the summit. But the key was still beyond our reach. Cloud blocked out the view of the way from the glacier onto the steep ridge. All we could see was an assortment of cliffs and crumbling ice-falls that seemed to hold no promise of success.

By the time we had reached the centre of the glacier that passed beneath the ridge, we had abandoned any hope of setting up our base camp here. None of us had ever seen such a dangerous place before. Weather reports we had received earlier from Alaska indicated that the amount of snow-fall in the area the previous winter was probably the lightest on record. The glacier confirmed this. Where one could reasonably expect a thick blanket of snow at this time of year, crevasses puckered their lips on every side. The weather was abnormally warm, and the strength that frost gives to the snow was conspicuously lacking. Crevasse edges would constantly crumble beneath us as the vast glacier defied most of the laws with which well-behaved ice is expected to conform.

It was eerie, walking just beneath the clouds and listening to the constant battlefront roar of avalanches that we could never see. When we rejoined the others, we learned that several of them had again dropped into crevasses while bringing in the rest of the bundles. So there was no difficulty deciding that camp had to be moved, and quickly. Seven hundred feet above, on a mound of rocks offering safety from the snow-slopes of the mountain side above, was a good potential site.

Sunday, the traditional day of rest, was an excellent illustration of why North Americans cannot be hired as back-packers, as can mountain people of some countries. They just would not stand for the work involved – and you can hardly blame them.

We had to move our whole camp up seven hundred feet on the steep, loose mountain side, and each man had to make three round trips. The first time, I carried four ration boxes, containing food for four men for four days, and weighing a total of forty pounds. On my second trip I carried over sixty pounds; on the final one I was afraid to weigh the pack. I could barely move. Yet most of the others carried more, particularly Denis, who yields little to the bears in the matter of strength.

The rock pile at 4,300 feet might have looked inviting to the marmots who whistled all around us, but it took the eye of faith to see comfort in it. Fips, however, is an architect and designer to whom anything but order is anathema. Quickly we all set to work levelling platforms for the tents. When we finished, Fips had us building patios at the entrances, shelter walls, and finally smooth, neat paths from the tents to the cooking area.

From the "kitchen", which consisted of two tea chests containing a two-burner stove and the pressure cookers, the view was almost overwhelming. To the west, the glacier streaming in rhythmic steps down to the silver-scaled ocean; at our feet, the chaotic beauty of the ice-fall, with sparkling turquoise pools in the hollows; and everywhere the flash of greens and blues from the glistening ice.

And to the north-east, Fairweather loomed, two vertical miles of ice and snow. Already, it seemed, our presence was causing it some discontent. Throughout the day it growled at us, occasionally roaring defiance as ice-cliffs on its face danced angrily and fell. The arm-chair traveller through far-off lands may smugly smile when he reads of natives who fear the mountain gods. But in places like this it is easy to credit the superstitious fear that attributes supernatural power to the garrulous rantings of an ice-clad peak.

Now we were established in safety and comfort, and it was time to get on with the climbing. The consistently warm weather worried us, for each day of it made glacier travel more dangerous. Later, we found that the surface did not refreeze even in the couple of hours of twilight that passed for night in these northern latitudes. So we decided that the next day we would all go up to the foot of the so-called Carpé Ridge and try to find a way onto it.

Fips, Paul, Joe, and Walter would put an overnight camp (Camp One) on the glacier, and try to establish a more permanent Camp Two at 9,000 feet or higher. Then they would make the first try for the summit.

The need for speed became evident as we moved out of base camp on Monday, June 23 – Fips's birthday. In the few days since our first visit to the upper glacier, the surface had become much worse. Four of us dropped through rotten bridges in the five hours we took to reach the foot of the ridge. Fips's party stopped about four hundred yards out from the edge of the glacier and set up camp on a small and spectacular spot. It was an ice-block about eight feet wide and twenty feet long, with deep crevasses on all four sides – the sort of place where one needed to keep one's eyes down and watch where one was stepping. But the temptation to look up was almost irresistible. All around us now were beautiful, unclimbed peaks.

And right in front of us, big, steep cliffs and bigger mountains of crumbling ice guarded the way to upper slopes that looked easier. There seemed no easy way, but we were looking at the route end-on, and there is no way of finding out the degree of difficulty on a climb without rubbing your nose against the problem. As my party set off back to base that evening, Fips and Paul went off one way, and Joe and Walter another, hunting anxiously for the key to the first big battlement door.

That night, the weather cleared, and at base camp the temperature dropped to a few degrees below freezing. What a difference it made to crossing the glacier! We reached Camp One with a load of supplies in a mere hour and a half, compared with five hours the day before. Everybody was still there when we arrived, and our hearts sank. Had they been turned back? Fortunately, one reason they were so late was that they had prospected until midnight before finding a way up. Another reason: one of the pairs had forgotten its stove.

We wished them well, and watched as they climbed a fairly safe fan of old snow and then vanished like ants amid the gullies in the rock cliffs. We pushed on up the main glacier, looking for routes up peaks we hoped to climb when and if Fairweather was in the bag.

Very soon we were a mile or more east along Fairweather Glacier in perfect weather. It seemed the sort of place that should be reserved for (morally) good mountaineers in the next world.

Mount Lituya (11,750 feet) was built of meringue-like masses of snow and ice piled dizzily one atop the other, promising almost a surfeit of snow-craft. To its west, Mount Sabine (named after Fips's daughter) lowered a fluted fin of ice right to our feet. As we watched, one avalanche from this peak fell a clear 3,000 feet through space before its debris billowed like smoke from the glacier. There is an exquisitely graceful air to a free-falling avalanche — but it is sobering to find at close range that the "tiny flakes" floating down through the air can be blocks of ice as big as houses.

To the north, Mount Quincy Adams, at 13,650 feet, was one of the highest unclimbed peaks left in North America. It obviously would not succumb to anything less than a first-class party. East of it was one of the most beautiful peaks we had ever seen.

Its classical summit, small in area, was supported by ridges of rock that were scornfully steep. Two others, about 11,000 feet, would be outstanding in almost any mountain range in the world. Small snow-fields clung to them at angles we all swore were impossible.

Every turn of the head, every slightly changed angle, every shadow from a fast-flitting cloud, served only to heighten the feeling that this was a special place in the mountains. It seemed almost too beautiful to desecrate with our unshaven presence, and was in itself adequate reason, if reason you need, why people climb mountains. Our constant stream of superlatives seemed thin and threadbare in the face of such grandeur.

We used adjectives of a different sort that night. As we reached base camp, clouds were filtering down the mountain sides to meet others boiling in from the sea. The next morning, we were sitting in the middle of a cloudy rain, listening to the cheery "ham" giving our weather forecast: cloud right up to 14,000 feet, rain and snow, and no sign of any improvement.

For a while our camp cleared, showing us a lot of new snow on the rocks above 6,000 feet. There was little chance that Fips and his companions would be climbing today – but the arrangement was for them to come down the next day and let us take our turn.

On Thursday, June 26, we moved up as planned, though nobody really expected the others to be coming down. Then, as we neared Camp One, the veil of cloud shivered and split, and we could see four tiny dots on an ice-field 5,000 feet above our heads. They were a day late, and had obviously made a late start that morning. By 9.30 they should have been several thousand feet higher than the 10,000-foot level they had reached.

Soon the clouds closed in again, and we approached the foot of the ridge. From some of the earlier accounts of the climb, we had assumed that Carpé and Moore had climbed this ridge, a little to the west of the route we took. In fact, neither of them had set foot on the ridge. Fuller research showed me they had in fact climbed a steep snow-face half a mile east of our route. Our routes joined just above the 9,000-foot level.

However, the fact that an ice-mountain has been climbed before means very little. Changes in the ice in a single season can make last year's easy walk a hair-raising climb, and vice versa. In more than a quarter of a century, major changes had probably occurred.

Now we kicked slowly up the inactive east edge of the ice-fall, to the west of the ridge. Once again, the nose-rubbing test proved the slopes not as steep as they seemed, though they were more than steep enough with our 45-pound packs. Almost 1,000 feet of this went slowly by; then suddenly we were on top of the cliffs. Ahead was an ice-fall, so we put on crampons, the iron spikes that make it possible to ascend steep ice without step-cutting. At 3 p.m. we came out of the clouds at 7,700 feet, and could see where the others had wandered onto a snow-face beneath some cliffs and pinnacles of rotten ice.

Now a stream of debris poured down towards their steps; so we kept clear and headed up a steep rock ridge. It, too, was rotten, and occasionally we had to remove our packs and haul them up after us on a rope.

How slow, how tedious it now became, and how desperately we equivocated to find excuses for stopping. Look at the view – take another photograph – tighten the crampons in case they came loose – what about the bootlaces? Any excuse would do, and nobody needed any coaxing to stop. The 600 feet up to 8,900 feet took us one and a half hours, but this was almost sprinting compared with the dispirited trudge that took us up the final 450 feet in the same time.

It was more or less chance that Dave spotted Camp Two, for nothing that even remotely resembled a camp-site had been visible on the continuously steep slope. And "Camp Two" was more a brave title than a place in which to relax.

It was just a spot where the plunging slopes paused for breath before hurtling headlong down again. A 500-foot slope of very steep ice came right to the edge of a cliff, where a few bare rocks showed through. Then the cliff dropped about 3,000 feet to a rutted glacier below. A big boulder protruded through the ice like a worn-down tooth at the rock line, almost as if its angry snarl was holding back the countless tons of ice.

In front of it was a ledge perhaps fifteen feet long, sloping down, and nowhere wide enough for the tents. Fips and his crew had humped dozens of small rocks to build up the ledge, but even then the tents could not be fully erected because the rock and ice got in the way.

However, the rock, by partly shielding both tents, gave an illusion of safety from avalanches that might swish down from the steep wide slopes above. When we arrived at 5.40 p.m., water was running out from under the foot of the ice-slope, which was very convenient for cooking. But the minute the sun moved around and left the spot in shadow, it froze. The narrow space along the edge of the cliff turned into a skating-rink.

For some reason, we were all reluctant to move out of the tents that evening, though the insides were a shambles, with pools of water and sodden equipment after a storm that dumped sixteen inches of snow on Fips's party in twenty-four hours. Our staying inside was doubtless based on the same magic principle that gives a child complete immunity from robbers or charging elephants by simply pulling a flimsy sheet over his head.

As we ate, cooking in a small area between the facing tent-sleeves, we wondered how eight of us would manage to preserve the social amenities while sleeping in two tents designed to hold two men each. As the evening wore on, however, we turned into our down sleeping-bags, easily rationalizing our selfishness with the thought that the boys had started so late they could not possibly get back until morning.

After a few hours of half-sleep, we were up before 3 a.m. preparing breakfast. Suddenly there was a splattering against the canvas, and I wondered for a moment if a slide had started above us. Pieces of ice began hitting the side of the tents in a torrent, and then we could hear faint voices. Several hundred feet above, the four climbers were chipping steps in the ice on the last lap down to camp.

It was almost 3.30 a.m. when they reached the tents, after more than nineteen hours of difficult climbing. All were tired, but bubbling with enthusiasm at their success. Said Fips: "What a mountain! It has everything. You think you are never going to get there. We first estimated we would reach the top at 4 p.m., then we changed it to 5. When we finally got there, it was almost 10 p.m. Just wait till you reach the wall of green ice near the top – Oh boy!"

Paul, with his lifetime of climbing experience, said simply, "It is a fantastic mountain. The best climb I ever made." Walter alone was a little quiet. His feet had been frozen, and he thought he had frost-bite. It turned out later that one big toe actually was frost-bitten, but the doctor snipped a little flesh off and there were no ill effects.

For a long time the mountain fairly rang with our excited chatter. Much of the rum bottle's contents gurgled into the coffee cups of Fips, Paul, Walter, and Joe; then we stepped out to leave them room to sleep. At long last, it was our turn.

When I was rock-climbing in the English Lake District, there was a constant grumble from rock-artists who had to walk for half an hour before they could express themselves on their favourite crags. These purists bitterly protested that energy not spent on serious, steep, and technical work was an utter waste.

From that point of view, even the purest of English mountaineers could not have complained about our Camp Two. We climbed out of bed, put on the rope, sidled six feet along the ice-covered ledge, and then stepped unsteadily up onto a wall of ice and snow. The 500-foot slope was one of the steepest of the whole climb, and finding it at the start of the day was rather too much of a good thing.

The time: 4.25 a.m. Our total of rest: very little. But our enthusiasm, for some obscure reason on which the psychologists need to do more research, was high. I have never had much use for the idea of slogging up a peak behind professional guides who were cutting all the steps, but this was the nearest I ever came to sympathizing with climbers who employ them. The steps that Fips's party had nicked down the slope were most welcome. It had frozen hard during the night, and the snow that covered the glacier slope was so firm that our crampons, with their store-sharp points, made hardly a mark.

It was exhilarating, and it is only in retrospect, as I see again our figures almost bouncing up the steep snow at that unearthly hour, that I realize Wilfred Noyes was right. After years of climbing in the Alps and the Himalayas, and just as many years studying his motives with an introspective poet's eye, he confirmed what my unimaginative friends had been telling me for years – that the urge to climb remains a flaw in the otherwise reasonable personality. His phrasing was more polite than theirs, however.

Our spirits were high as we pushed on, roped in pairs. There is a rhythm of motion, a harmony of step and action, that comes only at times when high training is joined with enthusiasm – times such as this.

Usually we moved together, but on steeper sections one would stop and pay out the rope around the shaft of his deep-pressed axe. There were crevasses everywhere, with morning-wide jaws, but the mountain was somnolent now, in a vast deep-freeze that stilled for a while the crumbling, sliding, melting of decay.

By 5 a.m. we had reached 10,200 feet, according to the small pocket aneroid I carried. By 7.30 we were almost 12,000 feet above the sea. At a time when human beings begin to think of breakfast, we decided to have breakfast too. But no breakfast nook in a modern, boxlike palace of gracious living ever had a view like this.

Three lonely fangs of rock pushed through the ice that had now almost completely enfolded our mountain. One was flat enough to hold the two small stoves, and, as breakfast drinks bubbled merrily away, we chewed on cheese and nuts and chocolate and watched the sun act as back-lighting to a gem-encrusted world of peaks.

The sun was clear, with no clouds to bar its rays, but the light that flickered from a myriad facets of the glaciers had no more warmth than the Northern Lights.

We went on refreshed, and the character of the climbing slowly changed. So far, it had been over wide and open slopes that made up the steep faces of the mountain. Now at last it began to turn to the slender, knife-edged ridge of snow that brings a tingle to the toes with every step. We arrived in the middle of a ridge, as our open slope faded into a long ridge gliding up from below.

Soon we were creeping up slowly, moving only one at a time with the speculative eye ever on the drop of a thousand feet to the left and even more to the right. It steepened, and, as I twisted in the axe and brought Denis up to lead on through, the sickle-edged curve of snow led my reluctant eye in a flash to the glacier 7,000 feet below. But the foot of new snow was well frozen to the ice, and our belays were safe.

A second similar arête of snow took us well up the mountain, and now the ridge had faded once again into the massive mountain face that gave it birth. The wind here had whipped the snow away and left a glistening sheet of bottle-green ice. It was just too steep in places for comfortable cramponing, and we chipped out steps that landed us on a luncheon platform at 13,500 feet. The time was now 11.30 a.m., and as our stoves roared away in a hole in the wind-swept ice, we could see signs not only of travelling hopefully, but perhaps of finally arriving.

While we had been climbing with our faces turned in to the steep slopes, some cosmic jester had been sprinkling the rest of the world with diminishing-powder. The peaks and towers that had loomed sky-high so long had finally dwindled.

For the first time in years I idly recalled – and promptly believed – what the geography master had said: that the world would be smoother than a billiard ball if scaled down to the same diameter.

This pleasant, idle cogitation made it no easier to climb slowly on. That eight hundred feet ahead of us now was no billiard table, but a sloping wall of rough green ice that wearily seemed to stay the same size no matter how far along it we trod, mechanically avoiding the blue-lined crevasse pockets.

It took forty-five minutes, each one longer than the last, to reach the top of the slope and find ourselves on top of the South-East Shoulder at 14,000 feet. The going was flattish now for over half a mile, and then headed up in a series of steps to The Nose, the thought of which had been niggling at our minds for hours.

Everybody still felt fine, with no sign of mountain sickness, but it was obvious that we had come up too far too fast and not allowed enough time to adjust to the thinness of the air. Nobody felt any real discomfort, but when we pushed the throttle down nothing happened. Our brave flow of movement had shrunk to a trickle. Each in turn stopped and sat, rummaging through his day-pack. We had brought only essentials with us, of course, but now, when the ounces counted, the "essentials" turned out to be a flock of unconsidered trifles.

Packs and spare clothing began to litter the snow, limp reminders of our arm-chair bravado, 1,000 miles away and 14,000 feet nearer the sea. I bitterly cursed the misguided enthusiasm that had led me to carry about nine pounds of movie camera and film to the summit, in case Walter's shots of the day before did not turn out. Naturally, not a scrap of the film I shot was ever used.

The four hundred feet of ascent to the bottom of the ice-nose took us one and a quarter hours, and as we reached it we could easily see why Walter and Fips, both craftsmen in ice-climbing, had chortled with glee when they spoke of it. They were chortling in retrospect, thinking of how the nasty Nose would knock the steam out of us.

Carved from clear green ice, it curved superciliously for about 150 feet before merging with a brow of cold grey cloud that suddenly appeared from nowhere. Grim as it looked, The Nose was the only line to take. On the right, ice-cliffs dropped sheer away with little prospect of climbing. On the left, steep ice thinly smeared with snow dropped to some ice-coated rocks and then bounded out of sight.

The wind was howling now, to remind us that we were getting close to 15,000 feet, where even a summer's day is arctic. Clouds whipped coldly past us as Denis hammered in a long ice piton and Dave led up yesterday's small steps, now jammed full of wind-blown snow. Slowly onward, each step an effort, and I tried the last steep move that would get us over the difficulty. Hand- and foot-holds nicked on a near-vertical wall of ice led around a fog-shrouded corner into a steep and shallow gully that faded upwards out of sight.

My courage then was on a par with my strength. At the awkward move from wall to gully I hesitated and was lost. Back I crept, ready to stop right there and leave the greater things to greater people. Once again Dave went ahead and vanished around the minatory corner. A few scrapes, some very quiet moments that seemed eternal, and the rope swung around to dangle vertically down the wall of ice beneath which we cowered. He was up. So, in a few more minutes, were we.

It takes but seconds to tell, though the doing took more than two hours. Now the aneroid said we were at 15,000 feet, with only three hundred feet to go if its indications were accurate.

They took us an hour of plodding, and when we reached the top the infernal little machine read 15,600 feet. The route wound in and out of the most impressive scenery. Turrets and battlements of ice, formed into fantastic shapes by the never-ending gales, stood guard around the big summit plateau, but fortunately we were able to weave our way easily among them. It was no effort for all of us to weave by now – in fact it would have been almost impossible for us to tread a straight line. Again, nobody felt unwell, but there was just no energy to call on. A single step often needed two or three gasping breaths.

We reached the top at 5.25 p.m., and as Russ's beard quickly vanished under a coating of ice, we realized we were not going to see much of this high point of British Columbia that we had come 1,000 miles to reach. The cloud flashed by in horizontal streamers, cutting visibility to about fifty feet. Not a rock was to be seen in the wilderness of snow and ice, and there was no way to build the traditional cairn anywhere near. I buried a rock piton in the snow, and after ten minutes of formal photography, mainly of British Columbia's centennial flag, we were on our way down.

The great moment we had dreamed about for more than a year turned out to be, like so many other "great moments", memorable only in prospect and retrospect.

For some of the descent, things were easier, as the pull of gravity was on our side. But soon we were tensed and working harder than we had on the way up. The beautiful snow arêtes, the essence of classical climbing, had crumbled in the day of steady sun. Now they were as stable and steady as porridge smeared on tilted glass. Each move was stilted, made individually, and "safeguarded" by a belay that was mainly psychological.

Slopes we rhythmically strode up in the morning took two or three times as long to descend, as the snow peeled limply off the underlying ice.

It was midnight when we reached the top of the last, steep slope above the tents. The strain of coming down, even more than the labour of climbing up, had wearied us. A maze of crevasses that we had crossed that morning on a bridge of faith and frost now tripped us up at every step. Denis and I were roped together, the biggest and the smallest in the party. Half a dozen times he broke into concealed crevasses. As I held him on a tight rope, he would half-swim out and flounder right into another. I was so tired that little flashes of light kept popping behind my eyes, and no tent in the world ever held so much promise of comfort and rest – and rest – and rest . . . .

Getting to it, however, was still quite a problem. The sun had long gone off the slopes, and they should have been freezing, by all the rules, for we were almost 10,000 feet above sea-level. They stayed like mush, and though we were over the viper's nest of crevasses, we still sank knee-deep at every step. Under this soft snow was ice into which the shaft of the axe could not be forced to make an anchor.

The slope steepened, and we caught up with Russ and Dave, who felt they could go no farther in safety – even though they were now only 350 feet from the tents, and in full sight of them.

I shared their feelings, and decided it would be wise to go back uphill to a comparatively safe spot and give the snow a chance to harden, making movement safer.

Then one of those odd things happened, of the type that occur only under conditions of great stress and fatigue, and, probably, a slight lack of oxygen. The late Frank Smythe has written of the time when, as second man on a rope of two, he turned to offer some food to the third man he felt had been with them all day. Others have talked to non-existent companions, and one wrote at great length about the old man of the mountains he quite matter-of-factly sensed on a peak.

No stranger appeared on my rope, but when quiet, competent Denis calmly said he would like to see what he could do, he began to grow before my very eyes. His voice deepened and boomed in my ears, and within seconds he was no longer just Denis but a huge, commanding figure. I had no difficulty accepting the evidence of my eyes that here was a giant rivalling those in fairy tales, and once I had accepted

154

it I thought no more about it. A giant had come along to help us out of a tough spot, and what could be more natural?

I let him down 120 feet until the rope ran out, and then he stamped and cut a hole through the snow to the ice. The ice itself was rotten, and in no shape to hold a piton if any real strain came on it. But Denis hammered one home; then, after we climbed down to join him, he joined both ropes together and fixed one end to the piton. The other he dropped right onto the tents. As calmly as if we were taking a Sunday stroll through the park, we all walked down, using the rope as a "safety" handrail.

We made only a quick drink when we reached the tent just after 1 a.m., almost twenty-one hours after we had left it, and fell quickly asleep. We left the piton and ropes where they were, as we were too tired to attempt to retrieve them.

About 9.30 a.m., the warmth of the sun on the tent woke us up. A few minutes later there was a gentle, slithering sound, followed by a metallic clang. The piton had fallen out of the ice, and our "safety line" slid gently down onto our sheltering rock.

The less said about the stumbling descent to base camp on Saturday, June 28, the better for our battered egos. Feeling very tired, and carrying heavy packs, including the gear Fips's party had left for us, we spent ten hours descending 4,000 feet. It was after midday when we left Camp Two, though we realized that the lateness would complicate our problem by softening the snow.

Proof of this presented itself the moment we stepped onto the main Fairweather Glacier at 10.30 p.m. A big snow-bridge we had used to cross one crevasse on the way up had collapsed. We followed the faint tracks of the first party, but they soon ran into another collapsed bridge. So we climbed down into the crevasse, fortunately a small one, and up the other side. The food cache was in a most precarious position. The block of ice on which it stood was melting rapidly, and canting a little. All the pitons holding down the plastic tarpaulin had melted out of the ice.

There was a rousing welcome when we reached base camp at 12.30 a.m. A bonfire was burning brightly, though it did not last long, as the fuel consisted mainly of cardboard boxes. A couple of the flares we carried for emergencies chased away the arctic twilight. As tall tales of our difficult peak followed the rum bottle around the circle, we spent two hours building the atmosphere of dangers shared and problems solved that makes most expedition members friends for life.

Next day we loafed, finding comfort on our rock pile and quietly studying our surroundings. The ocean was neatly packed in silver-white layers of long-ribbed clouds that delighted the eye. But Ken and George, at radio camp, were beneath them, and complained that it had not stopped raining for days down at the beach. Due south, a range of peaks little over 6,000 feet high stood stark of ridge and pregnant with ice. For hours we looked north at Fairweather and marvelled at how deceptive a mountain could be.

In the interests of accuracy for the taxpayers who were paying the bills, Fips's party scrambled up the rocks and snow above camp so that Mike and Kelly could shoot some photographs of them "nearing the summit". These were to fill in the blanks that Walter had left in the artistic whole, though he actually did take many shots on the summit and the approach to it. Fortunately, as these sequences were supposed to have been taken by Walter, he did not have to appear in them. He was able to stay in camp while Denis snipped off some of his frost-bitten flesh.

Our camp was certainly remote, but the peace normally associated with such remoteness was rarely evident. The scorching sun was speeding the tempo of disintegration, and always there was the thunder of avalanches. Many of them roared on for minutes at a time, and one was the biggest we had ever seen. Hundreds of thousands of tons of rock billowed down a mountain on the north side of the glacier, and bubbled like a chaotic flow of lava far out onto the ice.

While we were watching this primeval battle of attrition that had changed little in thousands of years, we were in constant touch with modernity. As Kelly lounged in breech-clout and sun-glasses, reading *The Theory of the Leisure Class*, Mike was on the radio, arranging to be picked up by Ken Loken, and for a hotel room in Juneau and a supply of fresh fruit!

The pilot was due to arrive on July 1, but even the best of radios cannot prevent human forgetfulness, and it was July 2 when he arrived. We rushed down the cliffs to our old camp-site and saw his little ski-plane a mile or so away, in the middle of the glacier running in from the south.

156

The crevasses were bad, and it took us some time to reach him. When we got there, we found he had dumped several cans of gasoline there as a mountain base, and was going to fly the boys out one at a time. It was awe-inspiring to watch him take off, bumping and swaying over the undulating surface of the glacier before staggering into the air.

He landed them, on skis, on a sandy beach about a mile from the radio camp. Then he flew back to Juneau, changed to a bigger plane on floats, and flew them and their equipment back to civilization.

It was odd, listening to him chat between flights, to realize just how true is the trite, tired old phrase about one man's meat being another man's poison. He nodded towards Fairweather with a big grin and asked how we ever acquired the nerve to climb such a mountain. He wouldn't even think of it, he said – far too dangerous.

Yet this assessment came from a man who made his living flying far-from-new single-engined aircraft in what is undeniably some of the most dangerous flying country in the world. In thousands of square miles there is nobody to help him if his motor fails. The weather is notorious for its rapid, lethal changes, and much of the time he flies completely alone. We shuddered at the thought. I shudder even more now that I have acquired my own pilot's licence. Eventually we each agreed that the other was a fool to tackle such dangers without some degree of alarm.

This time, however, the odds were on the pilot's side. The weather stayed perfect for flying, but all around us the snow and ice peaks began to peel and disintegrate in the unusually prolonged heat. Some of us attempted Mount Lituya, an unclimbed monster of 11,750 feet. I called that one off on a razor-edge of ice just two hundred feet below the summit. The rotten ice had a consistency of little more than granulated water, and I called to Paul as he hacked out ice-spray, "Let's call it a day. This is no place for the fathers of sixteen children to be." To get down we had to "swim" over rotten crevasse bridges, and avalanches were born of their own volition in front of our eyes.

All this had been great sport, but as we rested on July 4 we all agreed things had become far too dangerous to permit any more big climbs. The mountains echoed with avalanches, and we saw one that seemed to sweep over the site of our Camp Two, perched like an eagle's nest way up on Fairweather. As we returned to base camp, bridges collapsed on all sides and one climber muttered, "Let's get back to the beach. It's far healthier eating up strawberries than pushing up daisies."

We radioed to the Royal Canadian Air Force, asking them to pick us up on Thursday, July 10, instead of July 12 as planned. On Monday, July 7, we headed out to Lituya Bay.

Lituya Bay is about seven miles long and T-shaped. The short north and south arms of the T are fiords made by long glaciers that come right into the water. Great peaks rise from its head, and lesser peaks clad in forest and flowers flank both sides. The entrance is very narrow and may be used only at certain stages of the tide because currents boil through it at up to fourteen knots.

La Pérouse came here in 1786 on his voyage around the world. With infinite seamanship he pushed his sailing ships into the bay. He was overpowered by it and considered that the arms at the head probably led to the fabled inland sea of North America. In this he was rapidly disappointed, but he wrote in his diaries: "Its scenery has no parallel, and I doubt whether the lofty mountains and deep valleys of the Alps and Pyrenees afford so tremendous yet so picturesque a spectacle, well deserving the attention of the curious, were it not placed at the extremity of the earth."

He declared its harbour was equal to the finest in all France, and suggested that on the island in the centre French traders could establish a profitable trading-post. He suggested, too, that the Indian women of the local village — which no longer exists — were the most disgusting in the whole world.

The island in the bay is now called Cenotaph Island, a name bestowed by La Pérouse himself after a tragedy marred the splendour of his stay. Twenty-one of his men drowned when two of his boats overturned while they were testing the state of the tide near the entrance.

There was no thought in our minds of this tragedy as we came back to the peaceful bay that Wednesday. In a lily-dappled lake we had our first bath for weeks, ate bread that tasted wonderful despite the green mould on it, and listened to Ken's and George's tales of curious bears and monster fish. The plane was not due until 7 a.m. next day, so we had time to wander around the beaches picking spiny sea-urchin shells and other souvenirs for civilized planters a thousand miles away.

At 6 p.m., before we had even had supper, I heard the sound of Canso engines. The plane skimmed low and landed, and Ed Cameron urged us to get out as soon as we could. He was worried that there might be sea-fog the next morning, and he wanted to be safely in Juneau with us overnight. We cursed him roundly, but he would not even stop for a bite to eat. We whisked up trees to dismantle aerials, piled equipment helter-skelter into boxes, and hurriedly loaded the aircraft. I opened a can of stew with my knife and grumpily munched it cold on the beach as the rubber boat came in for the last load. At 9 p.m. we took off, just as several fishing-boats came through the turbulent entrance, seeking shelter for the night.

Two hours and seventeen minutes later, an earthquake and a mountainous tidal wave all but destroyed Lituya Bay. The quake was one of the most powerful in recent times, with a magnitude of eight on the Richter Scale. It was more powerful than the one that killed 10,000 people at Agadir, and similar to the one of Good Friday, 1964, that laid waste Alaska's cities. But the wave that followed was the biggest yet recorded anywhere in the world.

The cause of it all is well known to geologists — the Fairweather fault that runs right along the T-shaped head of Lituya Bay and under the glaciers on either side. Geologists who were flown to the scene measured a horizontal movement of the ground extending for 21½ feet, and a vertical upheaval of 3½ feet.

Eighty miles to the north, in Yakutat Bay, Mr. and Mrs. Robert Tibbles, who worked at the airport, and Mrs. J. W. Walton, a cannery owner, were having a picnic on Khantaak Island. Just as they were ready to leave, an enormous portion of the island suddenly reared into the air and then plunged under the sea. All three were drowned.

In Lituya Bay, a gigantic section of the mountain side at the head of the T was shaken off by the quake. Estimated to weigh ninety million tons, it dropped into the inlet and sent a jet of water spouting 1,700 vertical feet up the hill side on the north side of the inlet. A triangular section of forest a mile wide at the base was stripped to bedrock. When geologists inspected the apex 1,700 feet above sea-level they found whole trees hurled even higher up the slopes into still-standing timber. This, according to the United States Geological Survey, was eight times as high as any similar wave on record.

This awful wave raced across the inlet and then bounced from one shore to the other, compounding havoc and destruction as it went.

The farther it went, the lower it became, and the trim-line of timber, some of which had the bark stripped clean, sank gradually towards the entrance. But part way down the inlet, the wave surged over Cenotaph Island, which is several hundred feet high at the centre.

Three fishing-boats were at anchor inside Lituya Bay when the earthquake struck. Bill and Vivian Swanson were aboard the *Badger,* which was just inside La Chaussee Spit in Anchorage Bay just off our camp. Near them was the *Sunmore,* with Orville Wagner and his wife, Mickey, aboard. The 38-foot *Edrie,* carrying Howard Ulrich and his seven-year-old son Sonny, was anchored a mile away, near the southern shore of the inlet.

Mr. Ulrich wrote later in the magazine *Alaska Sportsman* that he saw the mountains shake and dance, throw clouds of snow and rocks into the air, and unleash great avalanches.

"I saw a gigantic wall of water, 1,800 feet high, erupt against the west mountain. I saw it lash against the island, which rises 320 feet above sea-level, and cut a fifty-foot swath through the trees of its centre. I saw it backlash against the southern shore, sweeping away the timber to a height of more than five hundred feet.

"Finally I saw a fifty-foot wave come out of this churning turmoil and move along the southern shore directly towards me."

Mr. Ulrich tried to pull in the anchor chain, but it would not budge. His account continued: "As the *Edrie* began her almost perpendicular ascent to the crest of the wave, the chain snapped and a short end whipped back and wrapped itself around the pilothouse.

"As we were swept along by the wave, over what had recently been dry land and a timber-covered shore, I was sure that the end of the world had come for Sonny and me and our boat. There seemed to be no hope for survival.

"I wanted my wife, back in the fishing village of Pelican, to know where and how her husband and her first-born had been lost and I grabbed the radiophone and yelled into it: 'Mayday, mayday. This is the *Edrie* in Lituya Bay. All hell has broken loose in here. I think we've had it. Goodbye.' "

Astonishingly, the *Edrie* survived. As the waves subsided, Mr. Ulrich escaped by what seemed to him an almost suicidal run through the narrows.

The Wagners, aboard the *Sunmore,* were killed. They saw the wave coming and tried to race it through the narrow entrance. It caught them, flicked them into the air, and hurled the boat over the spit and into the ocean.

The Swansons, quite incomprehensibly, survived the nightmare. The wave picked up their boat as if it were a matchstick, raised it fifty feet into the air, and bore it rapidly towards the spit. At this point, the spit is about two hundred yards wide, covered with huge boulders and trees.

The *Badger* flew right over the trees and boulders. Then she was dumped stern first into the Pacific. The Swansons had time to launch a dinghy before she sank, and were rescued hours later.

The only detail that remains to be told is what happened to our camp, which we had been so reluctant to leave. The Gilkey brothers, who knew we were due to stay the night there, flew down early in the morning to see if there was any sign of life.

The camp had vanished, the trees, the lake — all wiped from the earth in one instant of that night when the mountain fell. It was the sort of shattering climax which, had it torn some other range asunder, would have convinced the natives for ever that their gods were angry because the peak was climbed.